D1029402

WORLD OF ANIMALS

46

AMPHIBIANS AND REPTILES

LIZARDS 3

Skinks, Alligator Lizards, Monitors,
Worm Lizards ...

VALERIE DAVIES, CHRIS MATTISON

an imprint of
SCHOLASTIC

www.scholastic.com/librarypublishing

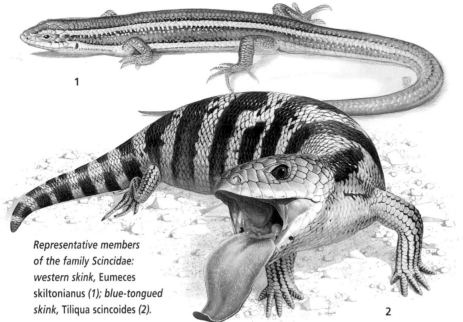

Representative members
of the family Scincidae:
western skink, Eumeces
skiltonianus *(1)*; blue-tongued
skink, Tiliqua scincoides *(2)*.

Published 2005 by Grolier, an imprint of
Scholastic Library Publishing
Danbury, CT 06816

This edition published exclusively for the school
and library market

The Brown Reference Group plc.
(incorporating Andromeda Oxford Limited)
8 Chapel Place
Rivington Street
London
EC2A 3DQ

Library of Congress Cataloging-in-Publication Data

Amphibians and Reptiles.
    p. cm. -- (World of Animals; v. 41-50)
    Contents: [1] Salamanders, newts, and caecilians / Chris Mattison -- [2] Frogs and
toads 1 / Chris Mattison -- [3] Frogs and toads 2 / Chris Mattison -- [4] Lizards 1 /
Valerie Davies, Chris Mattison -- [5] Lizards 2 / Chris Mattison -- [6] Lizards 3 / Valerie
Davies, Chris Mattison -- [7] Turtles and crocodilians / David Alderton -- [8] Snakes 1 /
Chris Mattison -- [9] Snakes 2 / Chris Mattison -- [10] Snakes 3 / Chris Mattison.
    ISBN 0-7172-5916-1 (set : alk. paper) -- ISBN 0-7172-5917-X (v. 1 : alk. paper) --
ISBN 0-7172-5918-8 (v. 2 : alk. paper) -- ISBN 0-7172-5919-6 (v. 3 : alk. paper) -- ISBN
0-7172-5920-X (v. 4 : alk. paper) -- ISBN 0-7172-5921-8 (v. 5 : alk. paper) -- ISBN 0-
7172-5922-6 (v. 6 : alk. paper) -- ISBN 0-7172-5923-4 (v. 7 : alk. paper) -- ISBN 0-7172-
5924-2 (v. 8 : alk. paper) -- ISBN 0-7172-5925-0 (v. 9 : alk. paper) -- ISBN 0-7172-5926-
9 (v. 10 : alk. paper)
    1. Amphibians -- Juvenile literature. 2. Reptiles -- Juvenile literature [1. Amphibians. 2.
Reptiles.] I. Grolier (Firm) II. Series: World of Animals (Danbury, Conn.); v. 41-50.
QL49.W877 2003
590--dc22   2002073860   Set ISBN 0-7172-5916-1

Project Directors: Graham Bateman,
                                Lindsey Lowe
Editors: Virginia Carter, Angela Davies
Art Editor and Designer: Steve McCurdy
Picture Manager: Becky Cox
Picture Researcher: Alison Floyd
Main Artists: Denys Ovenden, Philip Hood,
                                Myke Taylor, Ken Oliver,
                        Michael Woods, David M. Dennis
Maps: Steve McCurdy, Tim Williams
Production: Alastair Gourlay, Maggie Copeland

Printed in Singapore

About This Volume

This volume covers five families of lizards and the worm lizards, or amphisbaenians. Skinks form the largest lizard family and are found throughout the world. Most skinks are quite small and covered with smooth, shiny scales. They scuttle around in leaf litter and forest debris, and eat insects. There are exceptions, though—some skinks are large and rough-skinned, and others are tree dwelling or even semiaquatic. There is a tendency in the family for limbs to become smaller and to disappear altogether in some species. Skinks are also very adaptable and wide-ranging in their reproductive habitats. Adaptability is the key to their success.

The alligator and glass lizards are superficially similar to skinks and share many of their characteristics, including the tendency for limbs to become smaller and the occurrence of both egg-laying and live-bearing species. The two species of beaded lizards are the only venomous lizards in the world; the Gila monster, in particular, is a famous and fascinating inhabitant of the American Southwest.

The most advanced family of lizards is the monitors, of which there are about 50 species living in Africa, Asia, and Australasia. They include the largest lizard, the Komodo dragon, as well as a number of smaller but nevertheless impressive species. Monitors, called "goannas" in Australia, are intelligent predators and scavengers, quick to learn where they can obtain an easy meal. In many places they take the place of small carnivorous mammals.

Contents

The striking colors of the fire skink, Riopa fernandi, make this lizard a favorite with collectors.

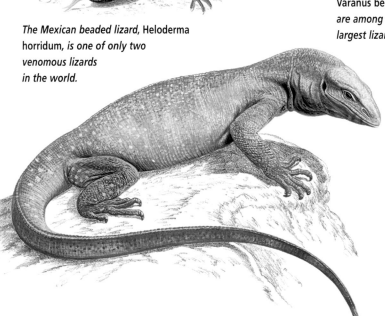

The Mexican beaded lizard, Heloderma horridum, is one of only two venomous lizards in the world.

At sizes of up to 6 feet (1.8 m) long, Bengal monitors, Varanus bengalensis, are among the largest lizards.

How to Use This Set

World of Animals: Amphibians and Reptiles is a 10-volume set that describes in detail reptiles and amphibians from all corners of the earth. Each volume brings together those animals that are most closely related and have similar lifestyles. So all the frogs and toads are in Volumes 42 and 43, the snakes are in Volumes 48, 49, and 50, and so on. To help you find volumes that interest you, look at pages 6 and 7 (Find the Animal). A brief introduction to each volume is also given on page 2 (About This Volume).

Article Styles

Each volume contains two types of article. The first kind introduces major groups (such as amphibians, reptiles, frogs and toads, or lizards). It presents a general overview of the subject.

The second type of article makes up most of each volume. It describes in detail individual species, such as the American bullfrog or the American alligator, or groups of very similar animals, such as reed frogs or day geckos. Each article starts with a fact-filled **data panel** to help you gather information at a glance. Used together, the two different styles of article will enable you to become familiar with animals in the context of their evolutionary history and biological relationships.

Data panel presents basic statistics of each animal

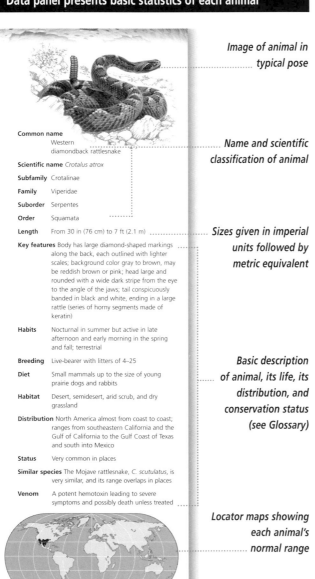

Image of animal in typical pose

Common name
Western diamondback rattlesnake

Name and scientific classification of animal

Scientific name Crotalus atrox

Subfamily Crotalinae

Family Viperidae

Suborder Serpentes

Order Squamata

Length From 30 in (76 cm) to 7 ft (2.1 m)

Sizes given in imperial units followed by metric equivalent

Key features Body has large diamond-shaped markings along the back, each outlined with lighter scales; background color gray to brown, may be reddish brown or pink; head large and rounded with a wide dark stripe from the eye to the angle of the jaws; tail conspicuously banded in black and white, ending in a large rattle (series of horny segments made of keratin)

Habits Nocturnal in summer but active in late afternoon and early morning in the spring and fall; terrestrial

Breeding Live-bearer with litters of 4–25

Diet Small mammals up to the size of young prairie dogs and rabbits

Habitat Desert, semidesert, arid scrub, and dry grassland

Distribution North America almost from coast to coast; ranges from southeastern California and the Gulf of California to the Gulf Coast of Texas and south into Mexico

Status Very common in places

Similar species The Mojave rattlesnake, C. scutulatus, is very similar, and its range overlaps in places

Venom A potent hemotoxin leading to severe symptoms and possibly death unless treated

Basic description of animal, its life, its distribution, and conservation status (see Glossary)

Locator maps showing each animal's normal range

Article describes a particular animal

Scientific name of animal

Common name of animal

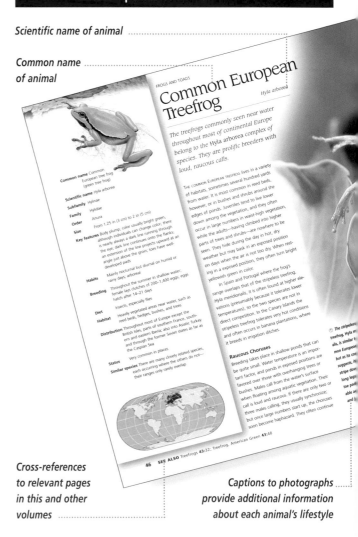

FROGS AND TOADS

Common European Treefrog

Hyla arborea

The treefrogs commonly seen near water throughout most of continental Europe belong to the Hyla arborea complex of species. They are prolific breeders with loud, raucous calls.

Common name Common European tree frog (green tree frog)

Scientific name Hyla arborea

Subfamily Hylinae

Family Hylidae

Order Anura

Size From 1.25 in (3 cm) to 2 in (5 cm)

Key features Body plump; color usually bright green, although individuals can change color; there is nearly always a dark line running through the eye; dark line continues onto the flanks; an extension of the line projects upward at an angle just above the groin; toes have well-developed pads

Habits Mainly nocturnal but diurnal on humid or rainy days; arboreal

Breeding Throughout the summer in shallow water; female lays clutches of 200–1,400 eggs; eggs hatch after 14–21 days

Diet Insects, especially flies

Habitat Heavily vegetated areas near water, such as reed beds, hedges, bushes, and trees

Distribution Throughout most of Europe except the British Isles, parts of southern France, southern and eastern Iberia; also into Asiatic Turkey and through the former Soviet states as far as the Caspian Sea

Status Very common in places

Similar species There are many closely related species, each occurring where the others do not—their ranges only rarely overlap

THE COMMON EUROPEAN TREEFROG lives in a variety of habitats, sometimes several hundred yards from water. It is most common in reed beds, however, or in bushes and shrubs around the edges of ponds. Juveniles tend to live lower down among the vegetation, and they often occur in large numbers in waist-high vegetation, while the adults—having climbed into higher parts of trees and shrubs—are nowhere to be seen. They hide during the day in hot, dry weather but may bask in an exposed position on days when the air is not too dry. When resting in an exposed position, they often turn bright yellowish green in color.

In Spain and Portugal where the frog's range overlaps that of the stripeless treefrog, Hyla meridionalis, it is often found at higher elevations (presumably because it tolerates lower temperatures), so the two species are not in direct competition. In the Canary Islands the stripeless treefrog tolerates very hot conditions and often occurs in banana plantations, where it breeds in irrigation ditches.

Raucous Choruses

Breeding takes place in shallow ponds that can be quite small. Water temperature is an important factor, and ponds in exposed positions are favored over those with overhanging trees or bushes. Males call from among aquatic vegetation, when floating among aquatic vegetation. Their call is loud and raucous. If there are only two or three males calling, they usually synchronize, but once large numbers start up, the choruses soon become haphazard. They often continue

⊕ *The stripeless treefrog, Hyla meridionalis, is similar to the Common European treefrog but as its common name suggests, the stripe down its long legs and toe pads is absent and…*

46 **SEE ALSO** Treefrogs 43:32; Treefrog, American Green 43:48

Cross-references to relevant pages in this and other volumes

Captions to photographs provide additional information about each animal's lifestyle

A number of other features help you navigate through the volumes and present you with helpful extra information. At the bottom of many pages are **cross-references** to other articles of interest. They may be to related animals, animals that live in similar places, or that have similar behavior, predators (or prey), lifestyles, and much more. Each volume also contains a **Set Index** to the complete *World of Animals: Amphibians and Reptiles*. Animals mentioned in the text are indexed by common and scientific names, and many topics are also covered. There is also a **Glossary** that will help you understand certain technical words. Each volume includes lists of useful **Further Reading and Websites** that help you take your research further.

Introductory article describes family or closely related groups

Graphic full-color photographs bring text to life

Easy-to-read and comprehensive text

Tables summarize classification of groups

Detailed diagrams illustrate text

Who's Who tables summarize classification of each major group

Introductory article describes major groups of animals

At-a-glance boxes cover topics of special interest

Meticulous drawings illustrate a typical selection of group members

Find the Animal

World of Animals: Amphibians and Reptiles is the fifth part of a library that describes all groups of living animals. Each cluster of volumes in *World of Animals* covers a familiar group of animals—mammals, birds, reptiles and amphibians, fish, and insects and other invertebrates.

The Animal Kingdom

The living world is divided into five kingdoms, one of which (kingdom Animalia) is the main subject of the *World of Animals*. Kingdom Animalia is divided into major groups called phyla. The phylum Chordata contains those animals that have a backbone—mammals, birds, reptiles, amphibians, and fish. Animals without backbones (so-called invertebrates, such as insects, spiders, mollusks, and crustaceans) belong to many different phyla. To find which set of volumes in the *World of Animals* you need, see the chart below.

World of Animals: Amphibians and Reptiles deals with two of the oldest lineages of land animals—the amphibians, which evolved from fish some 400 million years ago, and the reptiles, which evolved from amphibians about 350 million years ago. Although they are no longer dominant animals on earth (unlike the early reptiles typified by the dinosaurs), over 5,000 amphibian species and 8,000 species of reptiles can still be found. Most live in warmer or tropical regions of the world.

Naming Animals

To discuss animals, names are needed for the different kinds. Western diamondback rattlesnakes are one kind of snake, and sidewinders are another.

Rank	Scientific name	Common name
Kingdom	Animalia	Animals
Phylum	Chordata	Animals with a backbone
Class	Reptilia	Reptiles
Order	Squamata	Lizards, Snakes, Amphisbaenians
Suborder	Serpentes	Snakes
Family	Viperidae	Vipers and Pit Vipers
Genus	*Crotalus*	Rattlesnakes
Species	*Crotalus atrox*	Western diamondback rattlesnake

The kingdom Animalia is subdivided into phyla, classes, orders, families, genera, and species. Above is the classification for the western diamondback rattlesnake.

All western diamondback rattlesnakes look alike, breed together, and produce young like themselves. This distinction corresponds closely to the zoologists' definition of a species.

Zoologists use an internationally recognized system for naming species consisting of two-word scientific names, usually in Latin or Greek. The western diamondback rattlesnake is called *Crotalus atrox*, and the sidewinder *Crotalus cerastes*. *Crotalus* is the name of the genus (a group of very similar species); *atrox* or *cerastes* indicates the species in the genus. The same scientific names are recognized the world over. However, a species

⊕ This chart lists the phyla in two of the five kingdoms. The phylum Arthropoda makes up a high proportion of all invertebrate animals.

⊕ The main groups of animals alive today. Volumes that cover each major group are indicated below.

ANIMALS Kingdom Animalia		**SINGLE-CELLED LIFE** Kingdom Protista
Vertebrates/ Chordates Phylum Chordata	**Invertebrates** Numerous Phyla	

Mammals Class Mammalia	**Birds** Class Aves	**Reptiles** Class Reptilia	**Amphibians** Class Amphibia	**Fish** Several classes	**Insects, spiders, mollusks, spiny-skinned animals, worms**	**Single-Celled Life**
Volumes 1–10	*Volumes 11–20*	*Volumes 44–50*	*Volumes 41–43*	*Volumes 31–40*	*Volumes 21–30*	*Volume 21 (part)*

Groups of Amphibians and Reptiles

may have been described and named at different times without the zoologists realizing it was one species.

Classification allows us to make statements about larger groups of animals. For example, all rattlesnakes are vipers—along with other vipers they are placed in the family Viperidae. All vipers are placed with all other snakes in the suborder Serpentes; snakes are related to lizards, which are in the suborder Sauria, and so these two groups combine to form the order Squamata in the class Reptilia.

An important point must be made about the current scientific knowledge of these animals. New discoveries are being made every day, from the biology of individual creatures to the finding and naming of new species. Our knowledge of the relationships among the different groups is changing constantly. In addition, the number of species known increases all the time, particularly in the light of the very latest DNA analysis techniques that are available to zoologists.

Skinks

Family Scincidae 115–124 genera, about 1,400 species, but this classification is disputed and may be revised. Important genera include:

Genus *Acontias*—8 species of medium to large legless skinks from South Africa

Genus *Amphiglossus*—36 species of semiaquatic and aquatic skinks from Madagascar and other Indian Ocean islands

Genus *Carlia*—26 species of rainbow skinks from Australasia

Genus *Chalcides*—25 species of cylindrical or barrel skinks from Mediterranean countries and North Africa through to western Asia and India, including the three-toed skink, *C. chalcides*

Genus *Corucia*—1 species from the Solomon Islands, the monkey-tailed skink, *C. zebrata*

Genus *Cryptoblepharus*—29 species of wall or fence skinks from Australia, various Indo-Pacific islands, southeastern Africa, and Hawaii

Genus *Ctenotus*—95 species of striped skinks from Australia and 1 species from New Guinea

Genus *Dasia*—8 species of lizardlike skinks from Southeast Asia

Genus *Egernia*—31 species of smooth and spiny-tailed skinks from Australia, including the spiny-tailed skink, *E. stokesii*

Genus *Emoia*—74 species of slender skinks from coasts of Australia and various Indo-Pacific islands

Genus *Eumeces*—40 species of skinks from southern Asia, northern Africa, North and Central America, including the five-lined skink, *E. fasciatus*, and the Berber skink, *E. schneideri*

Genus *Feylinia*—5 species of snake skinks from Africa

Genus *Lerista*—79 species of ground-dwelling and terrestrial burrowing skinks from Australia

Genus *Mabuya*—124 species of terrestrial skinks from Southeast Asia, Africa, Central and northern South America, including the Cape skink, *M. capensis*

Genus *Neoseps*—1 species of burrowing skink from the United States

Genus *Nessia*—8 species of worm-eating skinks from Sri Lanka

Genus *Riopa*—4 species of forest-dwelling skinks from Africa and southern Asia, including the fire skink, *R. fernandi*

Genus *Ristella*—4 species of cat skinks with retractable claws from India

Genus *Scelotes*—23 species of terrestrial and burrowing skinks from Africa and Madagascar

Genus *Scincus*—3 species of sand skinks from North Africa and the Middle East, including the sandfish, *S. scincus*

Genus *Sphenomorphus*—112 species of forest skinks from India, Southeast Asia, Indonesia, and New Guinea

Genus *Tiliqua*—6 species of large, terrestrial skinks from Australia, New Guinea, and some Indonesian islands, including the blue-tongued skink, *T. scincoides*

Genus *Trachydosaurus*—1 species from Australia, the stump-tailed skink, *T. rugosus*

Genus *Tribolonotus*—8 species of casque-headed skinks from New Guinea, Solomon Islands, and New Caledonia, including the crocodile skink, *T. gracilis*

Genus *Tropidophorus*—25 species of semiaquatic skinks from Southeast Asia, Indochina, Malaysia, Borneo, and the Philippines

Genus *Typhlosaurus*—9 species of blind legless skinks from southern Africa

The family Scincidae has been described as the most species-rich lizard family. It has about 1,400 species in total, but there is some debate about the exact number of genera. Revisions are constantly being suggested, but the number is thought to be between 115 and 124.

The general description of a skink is a reptile with a flattened head, long body, tapering tail, overlapping scales, and short legs. However, there are many variations within the family. The head is often triangular shaped, and many species have an elongated or pointed snout. The top of the head is covered with large bony plates that are usually arranged symmetrically.

Although size and shape vary, most skinks have a cylindrical, elongated body with scales that are usually smooth, flat, and that overlap each other. In the New Guinea water skinks, *Tropidophorus* species, scales are keeled and roughened, while Stokes's skink, *Egernia stokesii* from Australia, has keeled, spiny scales.

The scales in skinks are supported by small bony plates called osteoderms. They are unusual in that each scale is made up of a set of smaller ones. (Other lizards have a single osteoderm in each scale.) This makes a strong but highly flexible structure.

Skinks' teeth are pleurodont, meaning that they are either fixed by calcified tissue to the inside of the jawbone, or they are located in shallow indentations in the jawbone. Teeth are lost and replaced throughout the skink's life, the new ones moving up from the tongue (lingual) side of the jaw to fill gaps left by any displaced

The casque-headed skink, Tribolonotus novaeguineae from New Guinea, shows the symmetrical bony plates on top of the head that are characteristic of the family.

teeth. As the skink grows, the number of teeth gradually increases. The tongue is fairly short, broad, and fleshy. It is slightly notched at the end and covered with flattened, overlapping tubercles.

The tail varies among family members. In some genera (*Eumeces* and *Dasia*, for example) tails are long and slender, up to twice the body length, while that of the stump-tailed skink, *Trachydosaurus rugosus* from Australia, is short and fat with a bulbous end.

Lifestyle Adaptations

Skinks are common on all continents of the world except Antarctica. They thrive even on some of the more remote oceanic islands. In Australia they are the most successful reptile group with about 370 species. The abundance of skink species in Africa, India, Indonesia, and Australia has given rise to the theory that the family evolved first on the southern continents and spread north and west.

Some genera have a very wide distribution and are found in both the Old and the New World. Species of *Eumeces* can be found in North and Central America, Asia, and North Africa. Similarly, *Mabuya* species inhabit Central and South America, Southeast Asia, and Africa.

Although most skinks have adapted to a terrestrial, burrowing, or subterranean existence, there are exceptions. A few species show specializations for an arboreal life. The lizardlike skinks of the genus *Dasia* from Asia, Malaysia, Borneo, and the Philippines are medium sized with long, gradually tapering tails. Most of them also have an enlarged, flattened area under the toes to aid climbing. Living in forested hilly areas in India, the partially arboreal cat skinks, *Ristella*, are the only species that can retract their claws into a sheath formed by a large, compressed scale. This enables them to move swiftly over the ground. The green blood skink, *Prasinohaema virens* from New Guinea, spends much of the day foraging in trees and bushes aided by toes similar to those of anoles and geckos. Just one species—the large and bulky monkey-tailed skink, *Corucia zebrata* from the Solomon Islands—has developed a prehensile tail, a useful adaptation for its arboreal lifestyle.

The slightly flattened tail of the keeled, or water, skinks, *Tropidophorus* species, is a modification to a partly aquatic lifestyle. These skinks live on the banks of streams and feed on insects and crabs. The diving skink,

Amphiglossus astrolabe from eastern Madagascar, has an unusual lifestyle—it lives in flowing forest streams. In order to breathe in this watery habitat, its nostrils are directed upward and situated a little higher on the head than in other skinks. Once in the water, the diving skinks move against the current to hide beneath rocks. They swim, dive, and prey on anything they can catch.

Cryptoblepharus boutonii is a terrestrial skink living on Madagascar and various islands in the Indian Ocean. It has adapted to conditions near the sea and can be found moving from rocks into the intertidal area to feed on insects, crustaceans, and small fish. Its periods of activity are regulated by the movement of the tides.

In Australia the rainbow skinks, *Carlia* species, spend most of their time on exposed rock faces. Therefore their limbs and digits are flattened as well as being longer and more slender. Other Australian species, for example, *Egernia*, are more robust with spiny scales that allow them to wedge themselves securely into crevices in rocks and tree hollows.

It is among the ground-dwelling skinks that most adaptations can be seen from a terrestrial to a burrowing way of life. Skinks that have moved to a subterranean lifestyle have also tended to protect, reduce, or even close the openings of their sense organs. Most of them have sunken eardrums, the opening of which is either small or closed to keep soil or sand particles from damaging the membranes. In the Berber skink, *Eumeces schneideri*, and the sandfish, *Scincus scincus*, the ear openings are protected by three scales.

Digit and Limb Loss

Adaptations to the digits, limbs, and head have also evolved as a result of the move to a burrowing lifestyle. Many skinks of the genus *Mabuya* resemble wall lizards (family Lacertidae) in that their limbs are well developed, comparatively long, and have five digits. In other members of the family Scincidae digits and limbs have been lost or reduced many times over the generations.

The skink family shows a gradual transition from lizards with four long, strong legs to the legless, snakelike lizards. Skinks of the genus *Ablepharus* have retained reduced limbs, but depending on species, they have lost varying numbers of digits from both fore- and hind limbs. Interestingly, the forelimbs never have more digits than

⊕ *In southern Australia the stump-tailed skink,* Trachydosaurus rugosus, *lives in desert grassland or sandy dunes. At night it finds shelter in hollow logs and ground debris.*

the hind ones (except in the Australian genus *Anomalopus*, in which the skinks have more fingers than toes). Eventually forelegs disappear altogether, and hind legs are the last to vanish.

The various stages of digit reduction and limb loss are seen clearly in *Scelotes* species skinks. Bojer's skink, *S. bojeri* from Mauritius, has four quite well-developed limbs all with five digits, while the black-sided skink, *S. melanoplura* from Madagascar, has four shorter legs, also with five digits. The silvery dwarf burrowing skink, *S. bipes* from South Africa, has lost its forelimbs. Its hind limbs are very small with just two digits. Finally, Smith's dwarf burrowing skink, *S. inornatus* (also from South Africa), lacks all traces of external limbs.

⊖ *Most skinks have movable, transparent lower eyelids that protect the eyes from dust and allow them to see when burrowing. This is a closeup of* Mabuya maculilabris, *the speckle-lipped skink from Africa.*

Movable Eyes and Spectacles

In most skinks a transparent lid covers the area of the lower eyelid. It protects the animal's eyes against particles of soil or debris when burrowing and allows it to retain some vision. The transparent lid shows different stages of development according to species.

The tropical ground-dwelling skinks, *Mabuya*, have a lower eyelid that is covered with small scales, a few of which have a transparent disk, or window. They make up the center of the lid. In the brown ground skink, *Leiolopisma laterale* from the southwestern United States, the scales in the center of the lid have slightly larger transparent disks. In the Travancore skink, *Lygosoma travancorium* from Asia, the window takes up more than half of the lower lid. In the lidless skinks, *Ablepharus,* from Australia, East Indies, Africa, South America, and some South Pacific islands, the window covers the whole lower lid and stays in place all the time. In this final stage it is known as a spectacle.

The fusing of the eyelid in this way is unique to skinks. Small, active, diurnal skinks in arid regions can lose moisture from the surface of the eye, which would be detrimental to the animal's well-being. By capping the eye with a fixed, clear spectacle, the problem is overcome. In temperate and more humid regions many skinks have a movable lid that encloses the transparent window. In a number of subterranean skinks the eyes are reduced in size. The spectacle also acts like a filter, decreasing the amount of light entering the eye.

For species such as the Southeast Asian snake skinks, *Ophioscincus*, and the South African dart skinks, *Acontias*, that live in almost complete darkness underground, the resulting impairment in vision is not a handicap. These species have also lost the external ear that detects airborne vibrations. Instead, they rely on vibrations transmitted through the semisolid earth to locate their insect prey.

The Australian genus *Lerista* contains 79 species of ground-dwelling and terrestrial burrowing skinks. They thrive in dry conditions in habitats ranging from leaf litter to sand dunes. All have minute ear openings and either an eyelid fused to form a fixed spectacle or a movable eyelid enclosing a transparent disk, or window. The genus shows progressive loss of digits and limbs from those with well-developed limbs and five digits to two completely limbless species. *Lerista viduata* is a terrestrial ground dweller that shelters among leaf litter at the base of trees and shrubs. It has well-developed limbs with five digits and a movable eyelid. *Lerista apoda* lives in the sand beneath layers of leaf litter and is totally limbless. Its tiny eye lies beneath a spectacle. Its snout is flattened and protrudes, making an ideal tool for digging.

As limbs degenerate in skinks, the tail alters so that for the greater part it remains the same thickness as the body. Since the legs are normally used in locomotion, legless forms change from walking to a snakelike, slithering movement. Assisted by the thickened tail, which is more powerful than a long, thin one, the body is thrown in horizontal curves.

Loss of limbs means that the head has to be used for burrowing. A broad, blunt snout would be useless, so in many burrowing species, for example, the sandfish, *Scincus scincus*, the snout is drawn out into a wedge shape or pointed cone shape. This adaptation is sometimes accompanied by an upper jaw that protrudes over the lower one as in the South African dart skinks, *Acontias*, and the Florida sand skink, *Neoseps reynoldsi*. The pattern of the head scales is modified to form a sheath around the skull, and the fusion of scales makes the structure of the head a more rigid tool for digging.

⊖ *The striped skink,* Mabuya striata wahlbergi *from Namibia, is more brightly colored than some family members. Its brown snout contrasts with the turquoise underside.*

Coloration

Although skinks tend to be various shades of brown, black, olive, and cream, many species have stripes, crossbars, spots, mottling, or blotches of differing sizes and thicknesses.

Skinks do not exhibit the rapid color change associated with chameleons, but some changes may occur as they mature and in the breeding season. For example, *Leiolopisma himalayana* males from South Asia develop an orangish-red band along the flanks in the breeding season. Members of the genus *Leiolopisma* also have colored tails—blue in *L. latrimaculata*, violet in *L. bilineata*, and red in *L. rhomboidalis*. The rest of the body is a dull brown. However, when these skinks bask in bright light, their scales give off an iridescence, and their

Tails—Use Them or Lose Them!

Skinks tend to rely on cryptic (disguise) coloration and the ability to disappear into the background to avoid danger. Many of them use an additional safety device, known as autotomy, whereby they can voluntarily detach part of their tail. While the predator's attention is distracted by the violently wriggling, disconnected piece of tail, the skink can escape.

Over a period of time the skink regenerates a new tail, although it is usually not quite as long as the original. Studies in the wild of the Great Plains skink, *Eumeces obsoletus*, have shown that the older the creature, the less likely it is to have an intact tail. Some species such as young Pecos skinks, *Eumeces taylori*, have conspicuously colored tails that add to their ability to distract predators. Not all species of skinks have a fracture plane in their tail (a point through one of the vertebrae where there is a special constriction to allow easy breaking); if a member of these species loses its tail, it will not regrow.

Having detached its bright blue tail, the five-lined skink, Eumeces fasciatus, scuttles away. The tail continues to twitch and creates a diversion. It will eventually regrow, but the new one will probably not be as long as the original.

① *A bright tail can be an asset in self-defense, as in the pink-tailed skink, Eumeces lagunensis from Baja California. Predators become distracted by the bright color and leave the skink alone.*

tail color stands out. Members of the genus often raise their tail and move it slowly from side to side, probably as a signal to warn off rivals and to attract a mate.

Diet and Feeding

Most skinks forage for insects, beetles, millipedes, small vertebrates, and plant and vegetable material. Collecting food is simply a matter of grabbing it in the jaws, crushing it with the teeth, and swallowing. The tongue is coated with sticky mucus that allows the skink to lap up ants and termites. Small species tend to have pointed teeth and are insectivorous. Larger species are more omnivorous. They supplement insect fare with plant and vegetable matter, including fungi. The Australian blue-tongued skinks, *Tiliqua*, are partly herbivorous, while, despite its size and stout build, the largest skink, *Corucia zebrata*, forages in trees for leaves and fruit. The teeth of herbivorous skinks are blunter than those of insect-eaters.

Any prey that struggles is held in the skink's jaws and banged or rubbed against the ground until it stops moving, after which it is eaten. Skinks of the genus *Nessia* from Sri Lanka have tiny, useless legs that cannot prevent their main prey item, earthworms, from sliding back out of their mouth. To overcome the problem and hold the prey in place, their teeth are pointed and curve backward.

Some species of skink are specialized feeders. Pink-tongued skinks, *Cyclodomorphus gerrardii* from Australia, feed mainly on slugs and snails. They have large, rounded teeth at the rear of the mouth that are used for cracking snail shells. Their specialized feeding technique involves approaching a mollusk while opening and closing their jaws and salivating. In this way their mouth becomes coated with a thick protective lining, allowing the skink to eat distasteful snails and slugs with no ill effects.

The mangrove skink, *Emoia atrocostata* from coasts around Singapore, swims and dives in seawater and feeds on crustaceans and small fish left in pools by the receding tide. A number of species of skinks will eat the contents of eggs found in the nests of ground-dwelling birds. On the Seychelles *Mabuya wrightii* uses its body to push the eggs of sea swallows from nests so that they fall onto the rocks below and smash. The skink scuttles down the cliff and laps up the contents.

Reproduction

Within the skink family all forms of reproduction occur. Some species produce eggs that develop in the female's body (ovoviviparous), others give birth to live young (viviparous), but about 60 percent of species are egg layers (oviparous). Live-bearing predominates in cooler areas or at higher altitudes where the incubation of eggs would be hindered by low temperatures. The advantages of warming the embryos within the female's body as she basks outweigh any mobility problems involved in carrying them.

In *Trachydosaurus rugosus,* the stump-tailed skink, one or two embryos develop in the female without eggshells and are supplied with nutrition from a placentalike organ. In the

genus *Mabuya* some species are egg layers, but others are live-bearers. The Indian skink, *M. carinata*, lays up to 23 eggs, but *M. multifasciata,* the oriental brown-sided skink from Indonesia, gives birth to six live young.

Sexing is not as straightforward in skinks as in other lizards, since, unlike members of the Iguanidae, the Cordylidae, and the Agamidae, they lack femoral pores (enlarged pores along the inside of the thighs). In addition, males have no head ornamentation such as horns or high casques. Nor do they undergo dramatic color changes, unlike the chameleons. However, male skinks usually develop a broader head as they mature. In other lizard families, such as the Agamidae and the Iguanidae, males use signals—inflated dewlaps, darkened beards, or arm waving—to intimidate rivals or to indicate submission without resorting to fighting.

However, when two male skinks meet, especially in the breeding

Care of the Eggs

Some skinks in the genus *Eumeces* have developed a type of brood-care behavior in which the female curls around the eggs, cleaning and turning them. It is thought that turning the eggs keeps the same part of the egg from being in contact with the damp soil all the time and prevents them from rotting. There is no evidence to suggest that the female actually uses her body to warm the eggs. It has been said that although the female guards her clutch and keeps away small creatures that would nibble the eggs, she will flee at the first sign of any real danger.

season, they rush at each other using their strong jaws to bite and tear flesh or limbs. Occasionally the injuries inflicted result in death. Similarly, when finding a female, there is no courtship display. Males track females by scent. If a female appears receptive, the male licks her with his tongue and uses his jaws to grab her side. If she does not resist, he grabs the nape of her neck or her shoulder in a vicelike grip. He then places one hind leg over the base of her tail. Slipping his tail under her, he aligns their cloacae to allow mating to take place.

Egg clutches vary in size from one to 30 eggs depending on species. Usually they are deposited in small holes dug under rocks or logs, in crevices, in the roots of shrubs, or in tree hollows. The site must be protected and subject to fairly high humidity to keep the eggs from drying out. Incubation varies from five to 10 weeks.

Generally live-bearers produce fewer young than egg layers. Large species do not necessarily produce large numbers of young. The blue-tongued skink, *Tiliqua scincoides*, gives birth to 10 to 15 young (although it has been known to produce 25), while the similar-sized and related stump-tailed skink, *Trachydosaurus rugosus*, produces one or two youngsters, each nearly half the size of the adult female. The monkey-tailed skink, *Corucia zebrata*, the largest member of the family at 30 inches (76 cm) long, usually has just one offspring.

⊖ *A female broad-headed skink,* **Eumeces laticeps,** *with her eggs in Florida. Females of this species usually lay between five and 20 eggs and remain with them until they hatch.*

Common name Monkey-tailed skink (zebra skink, Solomon Islands great skink)

Scientific name *Corucia zebrata*

Family Scincidae

Suborder Sauria

Order Squamata

Size Up to 30 in (76 cm)

Key features Head large; body stout and long with well-developed limbs and sharp claws; tail long and prehensile; color olive-green to grayish green with mottling; eyes green or brown but yellow in the subspecies *C. z. alfred schmidti*

Habits Arboreal; crepuscular or nocturnal; spends days in tree hollows; lives in small groups or colonies of several females and their offspring and 1 adult male

Breeding Usually biennial; 1 or occasionally 2 live young produced after gestation lasting 7 months

Diet Plants, including *Piper* species and *Epipremnum pinnatum* (family Araceae); some fruit also eaten

Habitat Primary rain forest with high humidity, especially areas where strangler fig tree is prevalent

Distribution Solomon Islands

Status Vulnerable (IUCN)

Similar species None

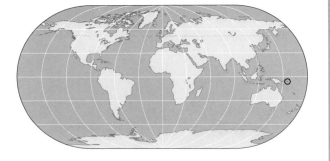

Monkey-Tailed Skink

Corucia zebrata

The largest member of the Scincidae, the monkey-tailed skink is also unique in having a prehensile tail. It moves slowly through the rain-forest branches using its tail as an anchor.

THE MONKEY-TAILED SKINK is often referred to as the zebra skink or the Solomon Islands great skink. It is the largest living member of the family Scincidae and is found only on some of the Solomon Islands (Choiseul, New Georgia, Isabel, Guadalcanal, Nggela, Malaita, San Cristobel, Ugi, Santa Ana, and Shortlands as well as Buka and Bougainville—the latter two being part of Papua New Guinea). It is common in lowlands and foothills up to 990 feet (302 m), although in the Guava area of Bougainville it has been seen at 2,970 feet (905 m) on the plateau.

The skink's habitat is tropical, mountainous islands that are volcanic and where daytime temperatures ranging from 79 to 86°F (26–30°C) are tempered by mild, southeasterly trade winds. Temperatures at night average 68°F (20°C), and humidity reaches 90 percent in the morning but decreases by the afternoon. Being near the equator, the islands experience little seasonal variation, although the more southerly ones have a slightly cooler season with humidity reducing to about 60 percent.

These tropical islands are covered by equatorial rain forest. The monkey-tailed skinks prefer the oldest trees in primary forest, including swamp and coastal habitats where the strangler fig tree, *Ficus* species, and *Casuarina* trees are present. With their dense foliage and extensive epiphytes (plants that grow on the trees) the latter provide the necessary shade and camouflage for the skinks. Monkey-tailed skinks are rarely found in secondary forests, which have few large trees remaining.

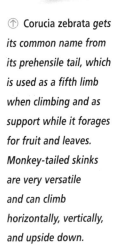

⊕ *Corucia zebrata gets its common name from its prehensile tail, which is used as a fifth limb when climbing and as support while it forages for fruit and leaves. Monkey-tailed skinks are very versatile and can climb horizontally, vertically, and upside down.*

Adapting to Life in the Trees

Although the monkey-tailed skink is large and heavy bodied, it is superbly adapted to an arboreal lifestyle. Its tail is prehensile and used as a fifth limb, allowing the skink to suspend itself while feeding or moving. It takes short rests in an upright position in dense foliage with its tail braced against the tree trunk or larger branches. When moving, it coils its tail around small branches. It is incapable of autotomy (tail loss)—a lost portion will not regenerate and would put the animal at a considerable disadvantage. The undersides of its feet have granular scales that are specialized for grasping twigs and branches, and it has sharp claws with which it can grip onto surfaces. It moves in a slow and deliberate manner, and this, combined with cryptic (disguise) coloration, helps the skink stay hidden.

Monkey-tailed skinks are active at dusk or at night for most of the year. However, during the wet period from January to April they are more diurnal, since the skies are overcast and there is no bright sunshine, which they avoid. Female monkey-tailed skinks are gregarious and live in small groups (or colonies) with other females and their offspring. The group is usually attended by one adult male. Areas with available food sources and tree hollows are claimed as core territories by a colony or a single skink. During nocturnal feeding the male patrols and scent-marks the area. The skinks spend the day resting in tree hollows, and they have been found in close proximity to possums.

Body Structure and Color

The monkey-tailed skink is easily recognized by its large, wedge-shaped head, blunt snout, and long, stout body with short but well-developed limbs that end in clawed digits. The head scales are irregular, and the frontal and nasal scales are pinkish. Body scales are relatively large and arranged in rows. The ear openings are almost as large as the eyes, and the lower eyelids are scaly. Dorsal coloration varies from pale olive-

green to grayish green. A combination of light and dark, almost black, mottling on the back and sides gives the appearance of stripes, hence the name *zebrata*. The tail, which is about 50 percent of the total length of the skink, is olive-green with a mottled pattern. The underside is a uniform yellowish green, pale grayish green, or cream. Individuals from Malaita Island tend to be darker.

The amount of mottling on individuals varies from island to island, which has led to suggestions that some should be designated as subspecies. At present there is a nominate form,

C. z. zebrata, and a subspecies described from Bougainville, *C. z. alfred schmidti*. Its status as a subspecies is based on its larger dorsal and ventral scales, the fact that it has seven instead of five parietal bones, and that its irises are bright yellow instead of green or brown.

Males appear to have large, broad heads and comparatively slim bodies, while females possess narrower heads and proportionately stouter bodies. Unlike some species, these skinks lack enlarged femoral (thigh) pores and preanal pores (above the cloaca), but mature males sometimes show a bulge behind the cloaca due to the size of the hemipenes.

Aggressive Courtship

Initial courtship involves both sexes tongue-flicking each other. Then the male shakes his head and moves his snout along the female's body. She moves away, and the male chases her. When he catches her, he bites her pelvic area and then grips her neck or shoulder region to subdue her. The bites are severe enough to leave scars that disappear only after several molts. Aligning his body with hers, the male uses a hind foot to stroke her pelvic area.

⬆ Monkey-tailed skinks range in color from pale shades of green or gray to darker shades, almost black in places. Although the body scales are large and arranged in rows, the head scales are irregular and tinged with pink.

➔ After an aggressive courtship, during which the male bites the female to subdue her, mating takes place. Female monkey-tailed skinks give birth to one or two live young.

This stimulates the female to arch her back and lift her tail, allowing him to mate. Mating usually lasts about eight minutes and takes place in trees, but the skinks do not use their tails to anchor themselves on a branch.

A few days after mating, the female spends three to four days hunched up—it is thought that ova are moving along the oviduct to the uterus during this time. Although the species dislikes strong sunlight, gravid female monkey-tails spend more time basking. The young develop and are nourished inside the female. About six and a half or seven months after mating, the female gives birth to one or occasionally two young skinks measuring 12 inches (30 cm). Birth usually takes place in a secluded spot and during the night.

Young Monkey-Tailed Skinks

When the newly born skinks emerge, they rest for a few minutes before consuming the birth membrane. About nine to 11 days later they molt and begin to feed on leaves. Eating the birth membrane enables them to survive until they shed their skin, and it also provides them

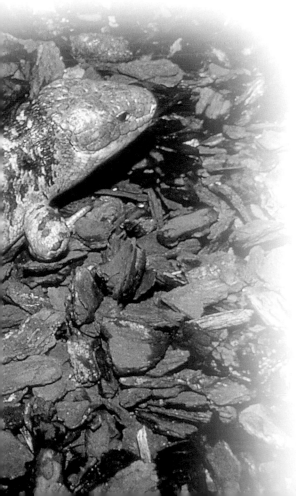

Specialized Feeding Habits

Although monkey-tailed skinks are referred to as herbivorous, they are primarily folivores (leaf-eaters) and feed mainly on the creeper *Epipremnum pinnatum* in the family Acaceae, *Pothos scindapsus* (Devil's ivy), *Piper* species (which are related to peppers), and new leaves of *Monstera deliciosa* (Swiss cheese plant). They also eat fruit but in smaller quantities. They may occasionally supplement their diet by lapping up the contents of eggs from birds' nests. Like a number of other lizards, they obtain additional nutrition through eating their own molted skin.

The monkey-tailed skinks are unusual among skinks since they possess an enlarged, partitioned colon, which is probably an adaptation to such a restrictive, leaf-based diet. The absorptive surface of the gut is increased, and food takes longer to go through. The colon contains a variety of microflora, which are important in helping digest so much plant material.

Other adaptations to such a specialized diet include extremely powerful jaws and short, cuspate (pointed) teeth. By specializing in this way, they compete less for food with parrots and bats, which primarily eat fruit. Studies in a forest have shown that dominant monkey-tailed skinks occupy the top layer of the canopy and that their feces are eaten by individuals below them, a practice known as coprophagy. This cycle continues to lower levels where foliage is sparser, and the monkey-tailed skinks at the bottom level become quite emaciated. As a result of coprophagy, some Solomon Island tribes consider the skinks to be unclean. Although they eat other skinks, they do not touch the monkey-tailed skinks.

with microflora in the gut that will be necessary for digesting foliage later on.

Females guard their young for between one and three months. Young skinks have been seen communicating distress to their parents and other colony members by breathing rapidly in and out through the nostrils and producing a chirping sound. The colony responds by grouping together to fend off danger. By the age of two most young skinks leave the colony. By leaving, food sources for the colony are preserved, and the dangers of inbreeding are avoided. The young skinks look for a territory of their own or try to join an established group.

Common name Three-
toed skink
(seps, barrel skink, cylindrical skink)

Scientific name *Chalcides chalcides*

Family Scincidae

Order Squamata

Size Up to 17 in (43 cm)

Key features Body extremely elongated; color varies from
olive-green to bronze, may be uniform or
have dark, longitudinal lines; lower eyelids
undivided with transparent disk; head conical;
snout blunt; ear openings larger than nostrils;
limbs and digits considerably reduced; 3 digits
on each foot; tail 1–1.5 times the length of
the body

Habits Diurnal or crepuscular depending on season;
hibernates for 4–5 months; basks to raise
body temperature before foraging for food

Breeding Live-bearer; female gives birth to 3–15 live
young; gestation period 3–4 months

Diet Insects, spiders, caterpillars, centipedes

Habitat Moist, grassy areas to drier, stony regions

Distribution Italy, southern France, Iberia, North Africa

Status Common

Similar species *Chalcides mionecton*; *C. sepsoides*

Three-Toed Skink

Chalcides chalcides

*At first glance the three-toed skink could be mistaken
for a snake with its long, thin body and serpentine
movement. However, its tiny limbs with three reduced
toes on each one give the game away.*

THE THREE-TOED SKINK, or seps as it is sometimes
known, belongs to the genus *Chalcides*, which
contains 25 species. Within the genus the limbs
of species vary from small to reduced with some
being almost vestigial. As evolution in the genus
has resulted in a reduction in limb size and
number of digits, the body has become more
elongated. As well as the change in body
shape, the number of rows of scales around the
middle of the trunk has decreased. The most
primitive species is *C. ocellatus*, which has five
digits on each foot and 26 to 34 rows of scales.
Chalcides chalcides has three digits on each foot
and 22 to 24 rows of scales. *Chalcides
guentheri* has tiny vestigial limbs, no digits, and
20 to 22 rows of scales.

Habitat and Behavior

The three-toed skink is found in a wide range
of habitats in western Mediterranean countries
and the Maghreb region of North Africa
(Morocco, Algeria, and Tunisia into Libya). In
fact, Morocco is believed to be an important
evolutionary center for the whole genus.

In Italy the three-toed skink inhabits grass
or clover meadows, and in northern Tunisia it is
found in open cork-oak forests. In other parts
of its range its habitat varies from herbaceous
vegetation up to 16 inches (41 cm) high to
reeds near lakes and salt marshes to shrubs on
moist ground. It is also found in fallow fields,
paddocks, and escarpments with dense grass
cover. In the Atlas Mountains it inhabits drier,
stony areas up to 7,590 feet (2,313 m).

Because of its shape people assume that
the three-toed skink is a burrowing, desert-

ⓘ *The three-toed skink
is very agile and can
catch flying insects. It
usually moves like a
snake with a winding
movement, but it uses
its reduced front legs to
pick its way over
hard surfaces.*

Persecuted

The three-toed skink is long and slender. When at rest, it rolls up and resembles a snake. Because of its snakelike appearance and superstitions that are associated with snakes, it has been persecuted by local people. The ancient Latin name was *seps*, which comes from the Greek *sepein*, meaning "to rot." It was originally thought that the bite of these creatures was highly venomous and that it would cause the flesh of the victim to rot.

dwelling species. However, unlike other skinks with similar shape and limb reduction (such as the Florida sand skink, *Neoseps reynoldsi*), it is terrestrial. The reduced limb size is an adaptation not to burrowing but to moving on surfaces with dense vegetation, where progress by serpentine movement of the body is easier than walking or running. The skink is very agile and can move through damp grass and thickets at considerable speed while barely touching the ground. During slower movement on hard or rocky ground it uses its tiny front feet and presses its hind legs against its body.

Until May the three-toed skink is active all day. During June and July, however, activity takes place in the morning in order to avoid the greatest heat. From August onward the degree of activity reduces—in September or October (depending on temperatures) the skinks begin hibernation

⊕ Closeup of the front part of the body of the three-toed skink. Because it is nonburrowing, its ear openings are larger than its nostrils.

that lasts until February. Much of their daytime activity involves basking in the morning with either the front part or all of the body exposed. When they reach the right temperature, they shelter under stones.

Body Structure and Size

The three-toed skink has a very slender, elongated body that is oval in cross-section. It has four tiny limbs, each with three toes. The largest specimen recorded was a female that measured 17 inches (43 cm), 11 inches (28 cm) of which was the tail. Its foreleg measured just 0.3 inches (0.8 cm) and its hind leg 0.5 inches (1.3 cm) long.

There are five subspecies: *Chalcides chalcides chalcides*, the eastern form, has shorter limbs than *C. c. mertensi*, the western form. The other three subspecies are based on

color variations. They vary from olive-green to bronze and can be uniform in color or can have several dark, longitudinal lines. There appear to be four dorsal pattern types that correspond to subspecies of the same name: *concolor* (uniform coloration), *vittatus* (four dark lines), *mertensi* (six dark lines), and *striatus* (11 lines). Specimens of all four pattern types can be found in Morocco, but *striatus* also occurs in Spain and the other three in Italy. The three-toed skink is occasionally confused with *Chalcides mauritanicus*, which lives in coastal sands, and with *Ophisaurus koellikeri*, the Moroccan glass lizard, which has no forelegs.

The snout of the three-toed skink is conical, and since the species does not burrow, the ear openings are prominent and larger than the nostrils. The lower eyelids have a transparent disk, or window. The body is covered with longitudinal rows of scales. Although not keeled, they are arched and underlaid with osteoderms (bony plates).

Insect Diet

Foods consumed by the three-toed skink include woodlice, centipedes, spiders, cockroaches, grasshoppers, earwigs, caterpillars, flies, and ants. Its feeding strategy is to observe

⊖ *The most primitive member of the genus,* **Chalcides ocellatus,** *has limbs that are not as reduced as those of the three-toed skink and has five toes on each foot. It is a fast-moving, agile skink that lives on scrubland, grassy slopes, and dry, sandy areas.*

Placental Development

The methods of reproduction in species in the genus *Chalcides* include both ovoviviparity (in which eggs develop and hatch inside the mother or hatch shortly after they are laid) and viviparity (in which females give birth to live young). The latter occurs in a number of other reptiles and involves the development of extra embryonic membranes next to the uterus. The three-toed skink, *Chalcides chalcides,* has the most advanced type of placenta. Not only does the embryo get water, nourishment, and oxygen from the placenta, its excretory waste is also taken away.

The same gene that is essential for placental development in mice has also been found in the three-toed skink, and its placenta has many aspects that are common to the placentas of mammals. Mature placentas of *C. chalcides* have been described as the most specialized found in any reptile, and they show a substantial transfer of nutrients from mother to fetus.

its surroundings with the front part of its body raised. Then quickly and deftly it shoots up from tufts of grass to catch the prey. When larger prey items are swallowed, it bends its head laterally in the same way as a snake. After lapping water, it holds its head horizontally.

Reproduction

Telling the sexes apart is quite difficult, but females tend to be larger than males. Research has shown that in many areas the skinks hibernate in groups at a depth of about 12 to 14 inches (30–36 cm). When they emerge after hibernation, males are particularly aggressive and will bite the necks and tails of their rivals. As a result of these confrontations, more than half of all adults and subadults have tails that have been regenerated.

Sexual maturity is reached in the third year. Mating begins from March onward, and females ovulate at the beginning of April. The gestation period lasts for three or occasionally four months, after which the females give birth to between three and 15 young. At birth the young measure 3 to 3.7 inches (8–9.5 cm). The number of live young depends on the size and age of the female, while their size at birth varies according to litter size—the more young produced, the smaller they are. Juveniles have voracious appetites and can double their size and weight in just a few weeks.

Predators and Defense

The three-toed skink shares its range with a number of predatory creatures such as the grass snake, the horseshoe racer, the false smooth snake, foxes, spotted genets, as well as egrets and aerial predators such as hawks and harriers. However, examination of the stomach contents of these predators reveals very few specimens of three-toed skinks, indicating that they do not seem to be particularly vulnerable. Their main form of defense is their agility and the fact that they are hard to catch even in low grass. Any specimens basking will evade their enemies by leaping through the air to land on another bush. If caught, many will twist and attempt to bite. The long, slender tail is very fragile; if necessary, the skink will cast it off to distract a predator and escape.

Common name Spiny-tailed
skink (Stokes's skink, Gidgee skink)

Scientific name *Egernia stokesii*

Family   Scincidae

Suborder Sauria

Order   Squamata

Size   10 in (25 cm)

Key features Medium-sized skink with flattened body
and tail; tail relatively short and sharply
tapering; 2 spines present on each keeled
dorsal scale, 1 large spine on each tail scale;
color and markings vary according to
location, may be reddish brown to dark
brown with pale or dark blotches or bands

Habits   Terrestrial, living in crevices or under rock
formations in colonies; diurnal, quite secretive

Breeding Live-bearer; female gives birth to 5–6 young;
gestation period 4 months

Diet   Range of insects and plant material

Habitat   Rocky areas in dry to semiarid regions with
tree scrub cover and *Acacia*

Distribution Western and central Australia; various
islands off the coast of Western Australia

Status   *Egernia stokesii badia*—Endangered (IUCN);
Egernia stokesii stokesii—Vulnerable (IUCN)

Similar species The pygmy spiny-tailed skink, *Egernia
depressa*, but that species has 3 spines on
each tail scale

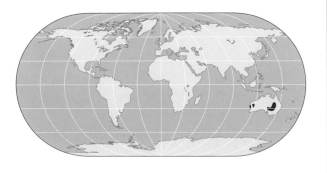

Spiny-Tailed Skink

Egernia stokesii

*A tail with spines is a useful tool for a rock-dwelling
skink. It can be used to snag against the rocks,
preventing the skink from being pulled out of a safe
hiding place, or to ward off predators.*

THE GENUS *EGERNIA* contains about 31 species
ranging in size from 6 to 24 inches (15–60 cm).
Species are divided into two types: smooth-
scaled skinks that inhabit grasslands, forests,
and sandy desert areas or spiny, rock-dwelling
skinks. *Egernia stokesii*, known as the spiny-
tailed skink, belongs to the latter group.

There are three recognized subspecies.
Egernia stokesii stokesii, the nominate form,
lives under limestone slabs on a number of
small islands off the coast of Western Australia.
Next, *E.s. badia* is found in the southwestern
interior of Western Australia and Dirk Hartog
Island, Shark Bay. The third, *E.s. zellingi*, is
found in the eastern interior of the country,
primarily in southern Australia and Queensland.

While the distribution of spiny-tailed skinks
seems widespread, populations are patchy in
dry to semiarid habitats. They are terrestrial
skinks, living in deep crevices or under boulders
in stony, hilly country and in mountain ranges.
Occasionally they use hollow trees if no suitable
rock crevices can be found. The rocky crevices
inhabited by spiny-tails are subjected to intense
heat from the sun and therefore experience
highly variable temperatures. By grouping
together, especially at night and during the
cooler months, the lizards cool down more
slowly—thermal control is probably the main
reason why they live in groups. They forage and
bask close to the security of their rocky crevices.

Body Structure

Spiny-tailed skinks have a relatively small head
and a robust body. The body scales are keeled,
and each dorsal scale has two spines. On the

tail they become a large, single spine on each scale. Young specimens are often mistaken for the pygmy spiny-tailed skink, *E. depressa*, but that species has three spines on each tail scale.

The sharply tapering tail is about one-third of the length of the body. Both body and tail are flattened, an adaptation that enables the skink to live under stones and in crevices. It can use the spines to its advantage when hiding in rocky crevices—the long, spiny scales catch on the rock surface and prevent the skink from being pulled out. It also uses its spiny tail in defense by turning it toward the enemy.

Coloration and markings vary according to location. Some individuals are reddish brown to dark brown with pale blotches forming irregular bands, while some are brown with darker and paler scales arranged in irregular, transverse rows. There is a population of *E.s. badia* that is completely black.

Spiny-tailed skinks are primarily insectivorous. They eat a wide range of insects, including grasshoppers, termites, and spiders. Their tongue is oval and flat, and contains a mucus-secreting membrane that enables the skink to keep a grip on insects. Fewer insects are available from mid- to late summer, and as a result, the skink's eating habits change at that time to predominantly herbivorous.

Closely Knit Groups

It is often thought that lizards show little social behavior except in terms of establishing territories and hierarchies. However, studies have revealed that the spiny-tailed skinks are among the most social of all lizards, capable of forming stable social groups and with a high incidence of long-term monogamy.

Spiny-tails form colonies of about 16 closely related individuals including adults, subadults, and juveniles. Maturity is reached only after five years, and most juveniles and subadults remain within their parents' social group for this period. Group members share rock crevices. They bask close together, often on top of each other, and defecate in common scat piles that seem to mark the group's territory.

Kin recognition—using chemical cues to recognize group members—is highly developed. Spiny-tails are able to differentiate between scats of kin and those of unrelated individuals. The social groupings provide two advantages. First, there is greater vigilance against predators; and second, the young receive high levels of parental care that increase their chances of survival.

Reproduction

Female spiny-tailed skinks usually give birth to five live young, each measuring 2.75 inches (7 cm), during February and March. The embryos, which are nourished inside the female by a placentalike organ, are born over two to three days. Research has shown that mothers and their young identify each other through the use of tongue flicks, and this recognition enables the mother to protect her young. Youngsters are particularly vulnerable, and the greatest mortality rate for these skinks occurs in the first two years.

It is not only the tail of Egernia stokesii that has spines. Each dorsal scales has two raised spines, giving the whole body a prickly appearance.

Common name Five-lined skink

Scientific name *Eumeces fasciatus*

Family   Scincidae

Suborder   Sauria

Order   Squamata

Size   Up to 8 in (20 cm)

Key features Body slender and elongated; body color
tan, bronze, or grayish olive-green with pale
stripes; juveniles have 5 longitudinal bright-
cream to yellow stripes on a black
background; tail is blue in juveniles and some
females but fades to gray in adult males;
head wedge shaped; ear opening distinct;
limbs short, each bearing five digits with
claws; scales smooth

Habits   Diurnal; terrestrial; may climb onto tree
stumps to bask and look for insects; also
burrows under rocks

Breeding   Egg layer; clutch containing 4–15 eggs laid in
a nest dug in moist soil; eggs hatch after
33–35 days

Diet   Insects, spiders, earthworms, crustaceans, and
small lizards

Habitat   Humid woods with leaf litter and tree stumps;
may also be seen around human habitations

Distribution Southern New England to northern Florida
west to Texas, Kansas, Wisconsin, and
southern Ontario; isolated groups may occur
farther west

Status   Common but listed as being of special
concern in some parts of its range, e.g., Iowa

Similar species *Eumeces inexpectatus* and *E. laticeps*
have similar colors and longitudinal stripes

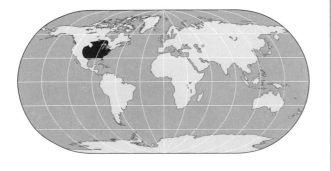

Five-Lined Skink

Eumeces fasciatus

Five-lined skinks can be seen in woods where there are plenty of logs, stumps, rock piles, and leaf litter. The brightly colored juveniles are more distinctive than the adults, whose colors fade with age.

THE FIVE-LINED SKINK IS PROBABLY the most common member of the genus found in the United States. Although its habitat varies, it prefers moist areas. It lives in wooded and partly wooded places as well as disturbed environments such as forest edges and cleared areas. It favors sites with wood and brush piles, stumps, logs, buildings, and outcrops, all of which provide shelter and basking places.

Five-lined skinks are diurnal and mainly terrestrial creatures, although they will climb onto stumps and small rotting trees to bask and search for insects. During the hottest part of the day in midsummer they often take refuge under rocks or logs. They are also accomplished burrowers and excavate dugouts under rocks. At night or when hibernating, they seek shelter in rotting logs, rock crevices, and sawdust piles.

They have a wedge-shaped head and a long, slender, cylindrical body. Males are slightly larger than females and grow up to 8 inches (20 cm) long, of which about 60 percent is the tail. The limbs are small but powerful with five clawed digits on each. The species can be distinguished from similar species by a middle row of enlarged scales under the tail and 26 to 30 longitudinal rows of scales around the center of the body. The skin is supported by small bones called osteoderms that lie beneath each scale, giving it greater strength.

Diet and Predators

Small invertebrates such as spiders, crickets, grasshoppers, beetles, millipedes, and caterpillars make up most of the skinks' diet. Snails and small vertebrates, including smaller lizards and newborn small mammals, are also

⊖ *The cream stripes and bright-blue tail indicate that this five-lined skink in Florida is a juvenile. The long, tapering tail can be broken off in the presence of a predator.*

eaten. The skinks are often seen climbing on houses and are regarded as beneficial, since they eat a number of insect pests. They crush food in their strong jaws prior to swallowing it.

The skinks rely on speed to escape from predators, including snakes, crows, hawks, racoons, and foxes. However, if it is grabbed, the skink can break off its tail voluntarily, a process known as autotomy. While the skink runs for shelter, the predator is distracted by the disconnected tail, which continues to twitch. The skink regenerates a new tail, but it is usually not as long as the original.

Reproduction

In spring the snout and jaws of mature males develop a reddish-orange coloration. Mating occurs between mid-May and the end of June, and females lay a clutch of up to 15 eggs some four to five weeks later. They prefer secluded nest sites under cover such as logs, boards, rocks, or partially decayed stumps.

They also prefer areas where the soil has a higher moisture content. The eggs absorb moisture from the soil, which enables them to

Bright Youngsters

Juvenile five-lined skinks are attractive animals with five narrow, longitudinal cream to yellow stripes running along the back from the snout to the tail. The background body color is black, and the tail is blue. A light-colored "v" shape on the head merges with the mid-dorsal stripe. The tail color dulls with age and turns gray, although some females may retain some of the blue coloration. Body coloration also changes to a tan, bronze, or grayish olive-green with pale stripes. In old males only faint traces of stripes may remain.

Male five-lined skinks will attack other males and smaller lizards. However, they do not attack lizards with blue tails. This enables both the adults and the juveniles to feed on different sizes of food in the same area and reduces the risk of juveniles being killed by aggressive, mature adults.

swell. Incubation time varies from 33 to 55 days depending on temperature. During this time the female coils around the eggs, feeding on any passing insects and exhibiting defensive biting behavior toward small predators.

She also regulates the temperature of the eggs by moving them up or down in the nest site; if there is a danger of it flooding or the eggs becoming too moist, she moves them to safety. After the eggs hatch, the female plays no further part in looking after the young.

Common name Berber skink (golden skink, orange spotted skink, Schneider's skink)

Scientific name *Eumeces schneideri*

Family Scincidae

Suborder Sauria

Order Squamata

Size Up to 18 in (46 cm)

Key features Head triangular shaped with pointed snout; eyes relatively large; body long and cylindrical with overlapping smooth scales; tail long and tapering; 4 well-developed limbs each with five long digits; basic dorsal color brownish or greenish gray; yellow-orange transverse stripes present on males and occasionally on females

Habits Terrestrial and burrowing; most of the time spent foraging on the ground but capable of disappearing beneath the surface or into water when danger is spotted

Breeding Female lays clutches of 3–20 eggs that hatch after 5–6 weeks

Diet Insects, sometimes small lizards

Habitat Variable, ranging from moist, grassy areas to semidesert

Distribution Northern Africa to Central Asia

Status Common

Similar species *Eumeces algeriensis,* the Algerian skink, but it lacks the lateral yellow-orange stripe

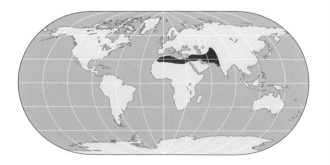

Berber Skink *Eumeces schneideri*

A ground forager, the Berber skink retires to its burrow during the hottest part of the day and at night. It is a fast runner and is not afraid to take to the water when fleeing from danger.

THE BERBER SKINK IS THE LARGEST member of its genus. Its taxonomy is a little confused. Some authorities recognize four subspecies, including the Algerian skink, *E. s. algeriensis,* but others believe that the Algerian skink is a species in its own right.

The distribution of the Berber skink includes countries in North Africa and the Middle East, Cyprus, Afghanistan, Pakistan, and northwestern India. It is often referred to as a desert species, but its habitat is far more variable and includes some quite humid and moist areas. These skinks can be seen in moist, grassy areas, in lush, herbaceous vegetation along ditches and oases, in drier bush and *Artemisia* steppe, on isolated sandy hills, on dry, cultivated land, and in semidesert. They emerge in the early morning and bask to reach a body temperature of 86 to 90°F (30–32°C).

Body Form and Color

The Berber skink is a robust lizard with four well-developed limbs, a cylindrical body covered with smooth scales, and a long, tapering tail. It has distinct ear openings and movable eyelids that lack a transparent window.

In adults the basic dorsal coloration is brownish or greenish gray. Males have golden-yellow to orange scales that form irregular, transverse stripes on the back and regular, transverse stripes on the tail. It is this coloration that gives the skink the alternative common names of golden skink and orange spotted skink. Females may have the same dorsal coloring as males or may be uniform in color. The underside in all adults is creamy yellow, and some individuals have gray speckling. A lateral yellow to orange stripe begins just below the

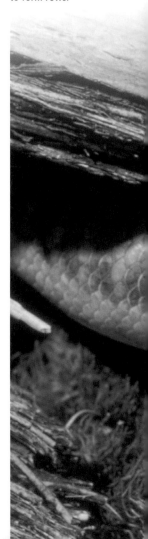

⊕ *The mottled appearance of the Berber skink comes from the irregular yellow-orange scales along its back. Further down the tail the yellow scales are arranged more regularly to form rows.*

Life On and Under the Ground

eye, runs through the ear, along the sides, and fades partway down the tail. The lateral stripe distinguishes *E. schneideri* from *E. algeriensis*.

Opportunistic Feeder

The swift, agile Berber skink spends much of its time catching insects, spiders, and smaller lizards. It is an opportunistic feeder and will also consume the young of small mammals found in burrows. It also supplements its diet with snails, using its strong jaws to crush the shells.

In North Africa two of the main predators of the Berber skink are the horseshoe snake, *Coluber hippocrepis*, and the Montpellier snake, *Malpolon monspessulanus*. Although the skinks usually rely on speed to escape predators, they will readily jump into water to escape from an enemy.

Courtship Conflict

During the breeding season there is considerable fighting. Males in particular may

Berber skinks lead a terrestrial and semiburrowing lifestyle. During the hottest part of the day and to avoid cold nights they retreat into large burrows. They either dig the burrows themselves between the roots of shrubs, using their strong limbs and claws, or they use burrows belonging to mammals. To prevent sand and dust from entering their ears, the skinks have three scales in a comblike arrangement at the front of the ear openings.

When its body temperature reaches 86°F (30°C), the skink's background color becomes lighter, almost whitish gray, since light colors reflect the heat. Unlike the sandfish, *Scincus scincus* from Africa, Berber skinks do not have scales between the fingers and toes and they are therefore able to move swiftly over the ground.

lose a leg or part of their tail as a result. Males attack any other individual of the same species on first sight, including females as well as rival males. However, they will use their tongue to probe and receive chemical cues; if the opponent is a female, they stop fighting. The male licks the female's cloacal region, and she reacts by raising a front leg, swaying sideways, and lashing her tail. The male grabs her tail base in his jaws and then delivers a strong bite to her side or neck before twisting his tail to raise hers and mate. The mating process lasts from seven to 10 minutes. Older females often bear the signs of scars from vicious bites inflicted during mating.

About five to six weeks later the female lays between three and 20 oval-shaped, white eggs under cover in moist soil. The female coils around the eggs to defend them from small predators, turning them to keep them from rotting. If the eggs seem to be in danger of drying out, she will either bury them deeper or urinate to moisten the area and the eggs. Once the eggs have been slit open and the young are beginning to hatch, she may also help them escape from the shell, using her mouthparts.

29

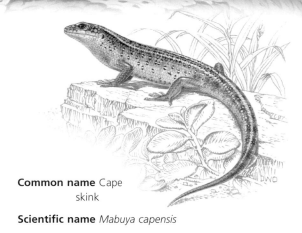

Common name Cape skink

Scientific name *Mabuya capensis*

Family Scincidae

Suborder Sauria

Order Squamata

Size From 8 in (20 cm) to 10 in (25 cm)

Key features Head with pointed snout; movable eyelid has large, transparent window; ear opening visible; body heavy; background color light brown to olive- or grayish brown with three pale stripes and cream and dark brown or black spots between the stripes; underside white or light gray; scales are cycloid (almost circular) and keeled; tail slightly longer than head and body length combined; spiny scales on soles of feet; females larger than males

Habits Terrestrial and diurnal; digs tunnels at the base of shrubs; basks in open areas

Breeding In most of the range females give birth to 5–18 live young after gestation period of 4 months; in 2 areas females lay a clutch of 6–12 eggs that hatch after about 2 months

Diet Insects, beetles, spiders, and worms

Habitat Very varied, including moist coastal bush, grassland, karroid veldt, and suburban gardens

Distribution Most of southern Africa except the Namib Desert and extreme northern regions

Status Common

Similar species Variable skink, *Mabuya varia*, has individuals that also lay eggs or give birth to live young depending on distribution and altitude

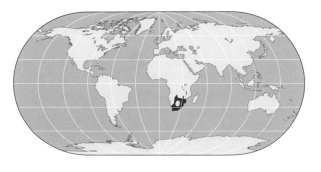

Cape Skink *Mabuya capensis*

The chunky Cape skink is probably the best-known lizard in southern Africa, since it is common in gardens and has an extensive range. Its stout shape has earned it the description of "obese" lizard.

MEMBERS OF THE GENUS *MABUYA* are often referred to as "typical skinks" since they have well-developed limbs with five digits each and relatively long, tapering tails. There are about 124 species distributed throughout the lowlands of South America and the Caribbean, Southeast Asia and the Pacific, sub-Saharan Africa, and the Indian Ocean.

The Cape skink can be found in most parts of southern Africa except in the western arid areas of the Namib Desert, the Kalahari Desert, the extreme northern regions, and Transvaal Lowveld. Relict populations exist on the Inyanga Mountains in the northeast of the region and the Limwa Plain in Zambia.

Cape skinks avoid the most arid parts of the subcontinent. They prefer moist, coastal bush, grassland, and mesic savanna. The latter is characterized by high rainfall, warm temperatures, and mild winters. The vegetation is a patchwork of succulent, moist thicket. By contrast, grassland occurs on the interior plateau at altitudes up to 6,930 feet (2,112 m). Although rainfall is plentiful, most occurs during the summer months. Trees are stunted due to the dry, extremely frosty winters. Arid savanna, also inhabited by the Cape skink, receives low rainfall, and winters are cold and dry. The differences in altitude and winter temperatures are determining factors in the skink's different methods of reproduction across its range.

Distinguishing Features

Other skinks in the genus have a typical elongated body, but the Cape skink is stout and has been described as "obese." A large scale beneath the eye (subocular scale) extends to the

⬆ *The need to bask for hours in the open makes the Cape skink vulnerable to predators. Like most skinks, it is ground dwelling and shelters in tunnels that it digs at the base of bushes or boulders.*

 SEE ALSO Skinks 46:8

upper lip and distinguishes this species from others with similar coloration that have the same distribution, such as the western three-striped skink, *M. occidentalis*. Its ear openings are crescent shaped with small lobes (scales) in front to keep particles from entering the ear when the skink is digging. The scales are cycloid (almost circular), each with three faint keels, although the keels are more pronounced on the dorsal scales. Another distinguishing feature of the Cape skink is the presence of spiny scales on the soles of the feet that help it grip stumps, logs, and rocks.

Background body color is light brown to olive- or grayish brown with three pale stripes. In between the stripes and extending onto the sides are cream and dark brown or black spots. Juveniles have more spots than adults. The underside is white or light gray. Occasionally uniform-brown individuals are encountered.

In order to pursue activities such as foraging for food, Cape skinks need to bask for considerable periods in open places to raise their body temperature to between 6 and 20°F (3–10°C) higher than the ambient temperature. As a result, they are active only on sunny days,

Egg Layers and Live-Bearers

The breeding behavior of the Cape skink is determined largely by location and habitat, and within its range individuals may be egg layers or live-bearers. In areas such as Pretoria and Port Elizabeth, which experience fairly high rainfall over much of the year and minimal seasonal temperature variation, females lay six to 12 eggs in November and December. The embryos feed on yolk during their development and hatch out from their eggs after about two months.

However, over much of the skink's range seasons are more pronounced, and periods of high summer temperatures are shorter. During the cold winter the skinks hibernate. Female skinks in these areas retain their eggs internally for four months, and the embryos are nourished by a placentalike organ. The females seek out and bask in the warmest places to aid their development. Eggs buried in these habitats would not experience high enough temperatures for long enough to be able to hatch. These females give birth to litters of between five and 18 young in March.

which means they are easily spotted by their main predator, the fiscal shrike. Cape skinks basking in suburban gardens have to avoid the added danger of cats. Despite their obese bodies, their well-developed legs allow them to escape quickly to their burrows.

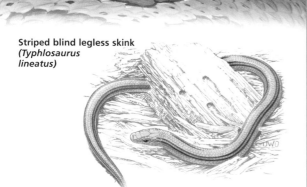

Striped blind legless skink (*Typhlosaurus lineatus*)

Common name Blind burrowing skinks

Scientific name *Typhlosaurus* sp.

Family Scincidae

Suborder Sauria

Order Squamata

Size From 4.8 in (12 cm) to 12.6 in (32 cm)

Number of species About 9

Key features Body long and thin with smooth scales; limbs lacking; large rostral scale on head; vestigial eyes present under head shields; no external ear openings; some species are light pink in color with a translucent underside; others are usually orange or golden yellow with stripes

Habits Burrowing and subterranean; spend most of the time below ground or under rocks and fallen logs; usually emerge only at night

Breeding 2 species are live-bearers producing 1 or 2 young; 1 species is an egg layer producing clutches of 3 eggs

Diet Termites and beetle larvae

Habitat Semiarid areas with sand dunes or sandy soils and sparse vegetation

Distribution Transvaal, Zimbabwe, eastern Cape, Mozambique, Namib Desert, Botswana, Namaqualand; 1 species in Zambia

Status Locally common, but *T. lomii* is Vulnerable (IUCN)

Similar species Giant legless skinks, *Acontias* sp.

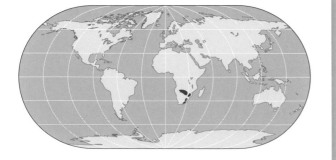

Blind Burrowing Skinks

Typhlosaurus sp.

Although not totally without eyes, the blind burrowing skinks do not really need sight, since their life is spent mostly below ground. When they emerge, it is usually at night.

THE GENUS *TYPHLOSAURUS* contains about nine species of blind legless skinks. They are endemic to southern Africa, although the striped blind legless skink, *T. lineatus*, reaches Zambia.

These small, blind burrowing skinks are mainly found in coastal sands and sand veldt, semistable sand dunes, vegetated ridges, and open sandy soils in grassland. One species, Cregoi's blind burrowing skink, *T. cregoi*, lives on montane, rocky hillsides and occasionally evergreen forest. There is very little rain in these semiarid areas, and the daytime temperature soars to 113°F (45°C), although at night it may drop to 41°F (5°C). When it arrives, rainfall is patchy; consequently only drought-resistant trees and shrubs grow in this landscape.

Night Tracks

All the species burrow in sand or under stones, fallen branches, or bark. They surface at night, and the only signs of their presence the next morning are thin, wavy tracks left in the sand. The skinks are rarely seen except during plowing or construction work, or when floods occur and they are forced to the surface.

There is little variation in color among the different species. Four members of the genus are light pink with no pigmentation and an almost translucent underside. Since they are subterranean and usually come to the surface only at night, they do not need camouflage coloring to disguise themselves.

The remaining members of the genus tend to be orange or golden yellow with stripes varying in number and thickness according to species. Cregoi's blind burrowing skink spends

Streamlined Design

Skinks in the genus *Typhlosaurus* represent the most extreme form of limb reduction in the family Scincidae—they lack limbs altogether. They also have other adaptations to an almost totally subterranean lifestyle. Since sight is not an important sense in their dark world, the eyes are almost lost, appearing only as vestigial dots under their head shields. The thin body is covered with relatively large, smooth, close-fitting scales that aid movement through the sand. The snout may be slightly flattened or rounded. The rostral scale, which is used for burrowing, is very large and oval shaped. At the front of the scale is a tiny nostril from which a groove extends. When burrowing, the nostril can be sealed by a plug that protrudes from the rear wall of the rostral scale. The external ear openings are hidden, preventing particles of sand or dust from entering.

⬅ Legless burrowing lizards leave snakelike tracks across the sand, as in this Roux's blind dart skink, Typhlacontias gracilis *from southern Africa.*

more time than other species at the surface and is normally gold with stripes, but individuals from the Transvaal are usually completely black.

Dangers Underground

All blind burrowing skinks feed on termites and small beetle larvae. Their broad, mucus-covered tongue is ideal for lapping up such tiny food. Despite spending most of the time underground, life is not without its hazards. For example, the golden mole, *Cryptochloris wintoni*, spends much of its life below the surface and uses its long front claws to kill blind burrowing skinks. Other predators include burrowing asps, *Atractaspis*, quill-snouted snakes, *Xenocalamus*, garter snakes, *Elapsoidea*, and harlequin snakes, *Homoroselaps*. The skinks have no defense against these enemies other than to move through the sand or soil at speed.

Due to their burrowing existence, little is known about the reproduction of blind burrowing skinks. The Gariep skink, *T. gariepensis*, and *T. lineatus* mate below ground during August and September. After a five-month gestation period one or two young are born. Studies have shown that it may be two to three years before they are sexually mature depending on location and food availability. Boulenger's blind legless skink, *T. vermis*, is thought to be an egg layer, since several females have been found each carrying a clutch of three eggs.

Common name Fire skink (common fire skink, Fernand's fire skink, Togo fire skink)

Scientific name *Riopa fernandi*

Family Scincidae

Suborder Sauria

Order Squamata

Size Up to 14 in (36 cm)

Key features Body cylindrical; limbs reduced; tail relatively long; blunt-shaped head; back bronze with red-and-black sides; throat and tail are black with white speckles; juveniles are black with red-and-gold markings, and their tail is black with contrasting light-blue rings

Habits Active by day; spends most of the time foraging in leaf litter or constructing series of tunnels

Breeding Female lays 3 to 4 clutches containing 4–9 eggs that hatch after about 65–75 days

Diet Insects, beetles, and spiders

Habitat Equatorial rain forests and plantations

Distribution West Africa (Cameroon, Togo, Equatorial Guinea, Nigeria, Ghana)

Status Common

Similar species *Riopa sundevalli*

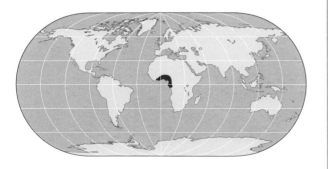

Fire Skink

Riopa fernandi

One of the most beautiful skinks in the world, the fire skink is popular with collectors. In its natural habitat it lives in the warm, humid tropical rain forests of West Africa.

OVER THE LAST FEW YEARS there has been uncertainty about whether the fire skink belongs to the genus *Lygosoma* or the genus *Riopa*. Most skinks of the genus *Riopa* are burrowers from Africa and tropical Asia. They tend to have long, cylindrical bodies, short legs, and long tails. The fire skink certainly fits that description. On the other hand, *Lygosoma* is a large genus containing a variety of skinks, most of which have slender, elongated bodies and reduced legs. Again, the fire skink would seem to be a suitable candidate for this genus. Some taxonomists place the skink in *Lygosoma*, some put it in *Riopa*, while others consider *Riopa* to be a subgenus of *Lygosoma*.

Fire skinks are widely distributed in the tropical regions of West Africa including Equatorial Guinea, Cameroon, Togo, Nigeria, and Ghana, extending as far east as Zaire and Uganda. They inhabit equatorial rain forests and plantations with a warm, humid environment. Humidity is over 80 percent for much of the year, falling to 65 percent in the cooler months. Daytime temperatures average 95°F (35°C), and even the nights are comparatively warm at 75°F (24°C). Fire skinks do not bask, which is an adaptation to living in a forest environment. They excavate a network of tunnels within the leaf litter at the base of trees, using their blunt head, strong neck, and long, clawed digits.

Body Shape and Color

At 14 inches (36 cm) in length the fire skink is one of Africa's largest skinks. It has a tubular or cylindrical body covered with weakly keeled scales. Its legs are small and have five digits with long claws. The lower eyelid is scaly and lacks a transparent disk, or window. The skink's

back is bronze with black-and-red sides. In some older males the sides are completely red. The throat and tail are black with varying amounts of white to bluish-white speckles, and the legs are black. Youngsters are particularly attractive and have a black back with red-and-gold markings. Their black tail has a series of contrasting light-blue rings that fade and eventually disappear as they age.

Fire skinks feed on a variety of insects and spiders. They move quickly through the leaf litter to catch their prey, crushing it in their strong jaws. They are able to sense the vibration of insects among leaf litter and will surface from their burrows to catch them.

When threatened, fire skinks initially open their mouth to gape and hiss before

⊕ *It is easy to see why* Riopa fernandi *is commonly known as the fire skink: The distinctive red-and-gold markings in juveniles give the impression of flames surrounding the body.*

lunging forward to deliver a sharp bite. Then they retreat into their system of tunnels. Their tail has a fracture plane and, if necessary, can be autotomized (broken off).

Reproduction

Males tend to have slightly larger heads than females and may have red coloration on the sides. There is no courtship prior to mating—the male simply pursues the female and grips her neck or her side just behind a foreleg. By sliding his lower body under hers, he lifts her tail then twists to align their copulatory organs.

Because they are secretive, little is known about reproduction in fire skinks in the wild. What is known has been learned from captive breeding. For many years they were thought to produce eggs that developed inside the female's body. Early attempts at captive breeding did not clarify the situation, since youngsters were discovered in the substrate, and it was not possible to say whether they had been born live or from eggs that had hatched. However, it is now known that they produce clutches ranging from four to nine eggs that they bury in chambers dug beneath rocks or fallen logs. Due to near-constant temperatures a female can produce three to four clutches a year. High humidity keeps the eggs from drying out, and it is thought that hatchlings emerge 65 to 75 days after the eggs are laid.

Myths

In parts of Cameroon the fire skink's bright-red coloration leads some people to believe that it is poisonous to the touch. In other parts of its range local people believe an encounter with a fire skink to be a bad omen. If they see one, any plans for the rest of the day are canceled in order to avoid accidents or mishaps.

Common name Sandfish

Scientific name *Scincus scincus*

Family   Scincidae

Suborder   Sauria

Order   Squamata

Size   8.8 in (22 cm)

Key features Head flattened; snout wedge shaped with countersunk jaw; scales smooth; toes have spadelike protruberances that act like flippers; tail laterally compressed and shorter than combined head and body length; color in adults yellow to brownish tan with yellow or brown spots or streaks and gray to tan transverse bands; juveniles are usually a uniform salmon color with a silvery-white underside

Habits   Diurnal, changing to nocturnal during the hottest months; hibernates in winter; basks with its whole body or just the head exposed depending on the time of day

Breeding   Female lays 1 clutch of 6 eggs at night in moist, sandy areas; eggs hatch after about 2 months

Diet   Locusts, ants, spiders, beetles, small lizards, insects, some vegetable matter

Habitat   Compacted and loose sand with vegetation

Distribution Northern Africa from southern Tunisia to Egypt to the Mediterranean coast; also in parts of Israel, Jordan, Iran, Iraq, and Saudi Arabia

Status   Common

Similar species *Scincus mitranus*; *S. albifasciatus*, the Senegal skink

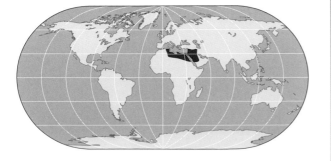

Sandfish

Scincus scincus

The sandfish is a unique desert skink that has adapted to a burrowing lifestyle. It can escape danger on the surface by "swimming" down into the sand.

THE SANDFISH INHABITS THE ARID African deserts, probably the harshest environments in the world. The Atlas Mountains form the northern limit of its range, and the skink can be found in Tunisia in areas up to the Mediterranean coast, parts of Libya, and into Egypt. It also occurs in Jordan, Israel, Iran, Iraq, and Saudi Arabia. It lives in compacted sand and accumulations of loose, drifting sands in areas with vegetation. It seems to prefer the edges of oases and the leeward side of dunes where there is less exposure to drying winds.

Its activity period changes depending on the season—usually it is active by day, but it switches to being nocturnal during the hottest months. In the fall showers of rain cool the sand, and the skinks prepare for hibernation, retiring to a depth of 8 to 12 inches (20–30 cm) near the roots of shrubs. Juveniles are the first to emerge from hibernation the next spring.

The sandfish needs to raise its body temperature to between 97 and 104°F (36–40°C) to be able to catch food. When the ambient temperature is lower in the early morning, the skink exposes its entire dorsal surface to the sun's rays. As the ambient temperature rises, it rests with only its head showing at the surface. Using the top 4 inches (10 cm) of sand, the sandfish can maintain its body temperature within a range of 98.6 to 104°F (37-40°C). During periods of excessive heat it retreats to deeper sand layers.

Life in the Sand

According to fossil records, the sandfish has existed for over 40 million years. It has a number of adaptations for life in the sand. Its

⊕ *Sandfish usually stay buried beneath the sand, but they surface to feed. These lizards live in very hot deserts and are active only for limited periods during daylight.*

skink to eat insects below the surface without taking in too much sand.

The spine and tail in sandfish are extremely flexible, so they can undulate their body while expending little energy. Both the back and underside are flattened; together with smooth scales, they give a streamlined shape that reduces resistance when moving through the sand. To keep grains of sand from wedging themselves between the scales and causing irritation, the scales are tight fitting and form an impermeable covering.

Unlike many other burrowing species in the family Scincidae, the toes are not reduced in sandfish. Instead, they are edged with serrated, spadelike protruberances that work in the same way as flippers in the sea and that aid the skink when moving through sand.

As in other burrowing animals, the sandfish has special protection to stop sand from damaging its sensitive organs. Preocular grooves in the face help guide sand away from the sandfish's eyes, which are sunk into the skull and covered with thick eyelids that are capable of closing tightly. In addition, the ear openings are protected by a covering of fringed scales.

broad snout and sloping brow make a shovel shape. By holding the head down and moving the snout from side to side, the sandfish can burrow quite quickly through the sand. When it wants to go deeper, it lowers the snout and raises it to "swim" to the surface.

The sandfish's mouth is streamlined and countersunk under the snout, allowing the

The Medicinal Skink

For many hundreds of years sandfish (or medicinal skinks, as they were called) and their feces have been regarded as a powerful medicine against many ailments as well as an aphrodisiac. Dried specimens, disemboweled and wrapped in wormwood, or just their ashes and fat were imported in large quantities from Cairo to Europe and regarded as a basic pharmacy ingredient until the later part of the 19th century. It was thought that their healing effect was due to the aromatic plants eaten by the skinks, such as wormwood. Some local tribes also prepare a beauty treatment from the excrement of the sandfish.

Coloration

The back of the adults has a yellow to brownish-tan background color, and each scale has small yellow or brown spots or streaks. Across the back there are gray to tan transverse bands. These bands alternate with the background color to provide cryptic (disguise) coloration. When motionless, the sandfish resembles the light and shade of ripples in the sand. Juveniles tend to be a uniform salmon color on the back with a silvery-white underside. As they grow, the yellow, brown, or gray color gradually appears to develop the pattern of the adult. This is unusual, since in reptiles uniformly colored juveniles rarely change into patterned adults.

Diet and Feeding

Sandfish can detect an insect moving on the surface from a depth of 6 inches (15 cm). They are able to estimate the weight, exact location, and direction in which the insect is traveling. When the sandfish makes its move, it breaks through the sand suddenly. With great accuracy it catches the prey and drags it under the sand. On the surface the sandfish is able to detect movement of prey up to 39 inches (100 cm) away. As it approaches the prey, it judges its size using binocular vision. Larger insects such as locusts are seized from the side and chewed. Once they are dead, the sandfish swallows them headfirst. Small prey items are seized in the jaw and then swallowed.

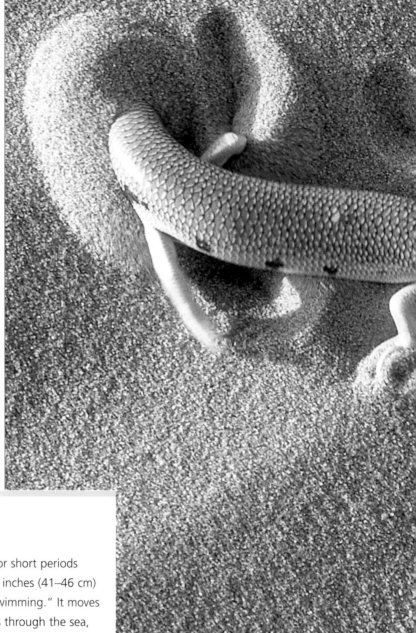

Sand Swimming

The sandfish runs on the surface of the sand for short periods only. It can dive to a depth of about 16 to 18 inches (41–46 cm) and uses a type of locomotion known as "sand swimming." It moves through the sand in the same way as a fish swims through the sea, using lateral undulation, but this is only possible in dry sand. (Attempting to move through moist sand where the grains stick together demands too much energy.) Even in dry sand the resistance of fine sand grains is considerable, so diving into the sand is mainly reserved for thermoregulation, catching prey, and escaping from rivals or predators.

Dry sand acts like a semiliquid and collapses behind a digging animal, but it does not penetrate hollow spaces from below. This enables sandfish to live under flat stones or among the root systems of plants. Since desert sand is lacking in silt, small spaces are formed between the grains, allowing air to flow through. While breathing under the sand, the sandfish moves its ventral surface up and down; when it exhales, a groove forms below the thorax. The position of the front limbs prevents sand from filling this air-filled groove, and the sandfish can continue to breathe under the surface.

A wide range of invertebrates such as beetles, other insects and their larvae, spiders, and scorpions are consumed. Sandfish occasionally catch and eat smaller lizards, especially *Acanthodactylus* species in the family Lacertidae. Although juveniles are insectivorous, adults supplement their diet with some vegetable matter. The flowers and young pods of broom, *Genista saharae*, are eaten in early summer followed later in the year by wormwood, *Artemesia absynthium*, and drinn grass, *Aristida pungens*. The adult's diet changes with the seasons and is mainly insectivorous in spring. When consuming plant

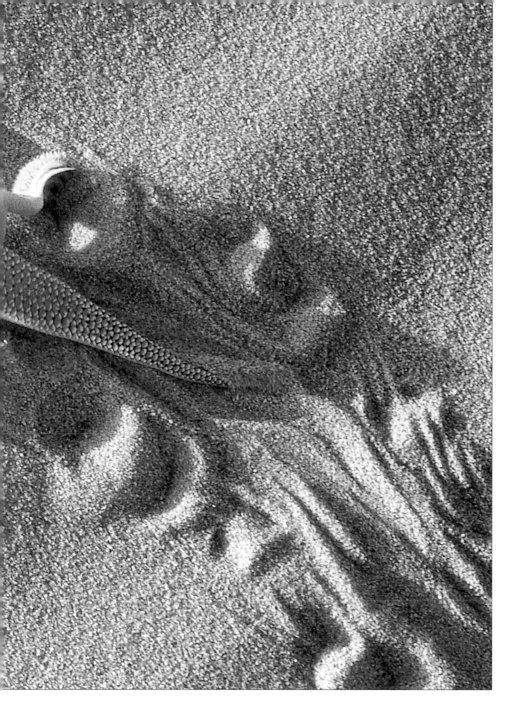

the skink was completely submerged was 0.41 seconds.

Humans also prey on sandfish. For desert nomads skinks are a staple food and an important source of protein. Hunting is usually a task given to children, who learn that the animal dives at an angle for a short distance and then stops. With time and skill a child can catch up to 50 skinks a day. If they are to be eaten immediately, they are roasted; otherwise, they are skinned, dried, and mixed with dried dates and kept for eating during caravan voyages.

Reproduction

Sandfish males grow larger than females. At the beginning of the breeding season in early May there is an increase in rival conflicts. As a prelude to mating, the male studies every sandfish he encounters. To find another individual, he investigates the sand by probing with his tongue. When he locates a sandfish, he approaches from behind. If it is another male, he attempts to drive him out of the sand by stabbing with his snout at the base of the rival's tail and then at the neck. This forces an inferior male to flee.

⬆ *With its wedge-shaped snout and streamlined body the sandfish is extremely adept at moving through its desert environment, literally "swimming" through loose sand.*

material, the sandfish also ingests sand, which is probably retained in the gut to help in the grinding process.

Hazards and Defense

The main predators on the sandfish are the desert monitor, *Varanus griseus*, members of the crow family, fennec foxes, and horned vipers, *Cerastes cerastes*. The latter holds on to its prey with a firm grip until it is dead, preventing it from diving down into the sand. Otherwise, the sandfish dives into the sand at the slightest sign of danger. During a series of experiments the shortest time measured until

When he locates a female, the male rubs his head along her body to persuade her to rise to the surface. If she is unreceptive, she flees. Otherwise, she remains motionless on the surface and allows the male to grip her neck. She then bends her body and lifts her tail, enabling them to mate. Afterward, the male cleans sand from his hemipenes by licking them or dragging them over flat stones. A clutch of eggs is laid usually at night among the roots of shrubs where there is more moisture. The young hatch out about two months later.

Common name Blue-tongued skink

Scientific name *Tiliqua scincoides*

Family   Scincidae

Suborder   Sauria

Order   Squamata

Size   Up to 24 in (60 cm)

Key features Head large; lower eyelid movable without a transparent window; body stout and flattened across the back from side to side; scales smooth; limbs relatively short but well developed; color varies according to subspecies, usually gray to tan or silver background with bands extending onto the sides; some have a dark streak running from the eye to the top of the ear opening; tongue blue

Habits   Diurnal ground dweller, usually slow moving; spends a lot of time basking and foraging for food

Breeding   Live-bearer; female gives birth to up to 25 young; gestation period about 110 days

Diet   Omnivorous; eats insects, fruit, berries, flowers, even carrion

Habitat   Temperate forests, subhumid forests, grassland, suburban gardens

Distribution Eastern and northern Australia and Irian Jaya (Indonesia)

Status   Common

Similar species Centralian blue-tongued skink, *Tiliqua multifasciata*; western blue-tongued skink, *T. occipitalis*; blotched blue-tongued skink, *T. nigrolutea*; pygmy blue-tongued skink, *T. adelaidensis*; New Guinea blue-tongued skink, *T. gigas*

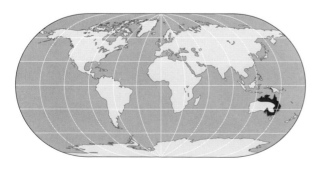

Blue-Tongued Skink

Tiliqua scincoides

The slow-moving blue-tongued skinks in the genus Tiliqua *are probably the most familiar of all Australian lizards. As their common name suggests, they have bright blue tongues.*

THERE ARE FOUR SUBSPECIES of *Tiliqua scincoides*. The eastern (or common) blue-tongued skink, *T. s. scincoides*, is the nominate form. It usually has a gray to tan background coloration with darker bands extending onto its flanks. Its forelimbs are plain. A dark temporal streak runs from the eye to the top of the ear opening. The northern blue-tongued skink, *T. s. intermedia*, is the largest member of the genus at 24 inches (60 cm) long. It is paler than the nominate form, the dark bands on its flanks are more orange, and its grayish-tan head lacks the temporal streak. The Tanimbar blue-tongued skink, *T. s. chimaerea*, is banded with golden brown and silver on the flanks. Its back is silver banded with gray. A fourth subspecies has yet to be officially classified but is referred to as the Irian Jaya form. Its head colors are similar to those of the northern blue-tongued skink, while the bold bands on its back are similar to those of the eastern form. It has a longer tail, and its forelimbs are dark brown with cream flecks.

Terrestrial Habitats

Blue-tongued skinks inhabit Australia, various Indonesian islands, and New Guinea. Although location and habitat vary depending on subspecies, they are all diurnal and have adapted to a terrestrial lifestyle. They often shelter in animal burrows, hollow logs, leaf litter, or rock crevices. The range of the eastern blue-tongued skink is southeastern Australia up along the east coast to the tip of Cape York Peninsula. It includes semiscrub, woodland, and coastal habitats. The northern blue-tongued skink inhabits drier open woodlands and

⊙ *When threatened, the blue-tongued skink puffs up its body, sticks out its long blue tongue, and hisses. The bright tongue contrasts with the pink mouth lining and acts as a warning to predators.*

Suburban Skinks

subhumid forests. It ranges from Western Australia along the northern coast through Northern Territory and into Queensland. The smaller-sized subspecies *T. s. chimaerea* inhabits subhumid and tropical forests on the Tanimbar Islands off the northern coast of Australia. The Irian Jaya blue-tongued skink is found in drier tropical regions of southern coastal New Guinea where climate and vegetation are similar to adjacent northern Australia.

Activity periods for blue-tongued skinks vary with habitat and temperature. Individuals in northern parts tend to be active mostly in the early morning and later afternoon, seeking burrows in which to spend the hottest part of the day. Blue-tongued skinks are ectotherms. They bask to raise their body temperature to 95° F (35°C). They are unusual among skinks in that they pant to cool down. During this process they open their mouth when inhaling and close it when exhaling (unlike other

More than any other blue-tongued skink, the eastern (or common) form, *T. s. scincoides*, thrives in urban areas and reaches the suburbs of most cities within its range. It has adapted to large gardens with plenty of shelter, making its home in rockeries, pipes, and cavities under houses. Lawns and paths make useful basking sites. Although the skink has become used to human activity, life in suburbia is not without its hazards. A number of adults, especially males, tend to be killed by dogs and motor vehicles in spring (the mating season) when they move around more frequently. Later in the year most deaths occur among young that are preyed on by cats. In addition, chemicals used to control snail and slug populations in gardens have killed numbers of blue-tongued skinks.

Research has shown that the skinks use corridors of dense vegetation to move between retreat sites. Females, especially gravid individuals, are highly sedentary and often use the same site for 10 or more years. Their habit of returning to the same site, combined with adequate food supplies in the form of snails, slugs, caterpillars, fruits, and plants, and a long life span mean that populations of adult blue-tongued skinks in suburbia are stable.

panting lizards, which hold the mouth open all the time). During the dry season when food and water are limited, they conserve energy levels by staying in their burrows and allowing their body temperature to fall, which lowers their metabolic rate.

Body Features

The blue-tongued skink is among the largest in the skink family. Its body is long and flattened with small legs, each with short-clawed digits. The tail is about 50 to 60 percent of the head and body length, tapering sharply at the tip. When moving in thick vegetation, the skink folds its hind limbs back along the tail and uses lateral undulation. The limbs and claws are not strong enough for the skink to dig its own burrow, so it uses those of mammals. The skink's head is quite large. It has prominent ear openings with small scales in front. It has strong jaws and a wide gape. The teeth at the front of the mouth are smaller than those farther along the jaw and are used to pick off insects and to bite plant material. The tongue is, of course, blue. It is also large and broad.

Blue-tongued skinks are opportunistic feeders. They rely on prey that is slower than themselves. Insects, fruit, flowers, foliage, fungi, snails, eggs, small vertebrates, and carrion are all eaten. When feeding on insects and snails, the skink captures its prey and crushes it in its jaws before swallowing. Consumption of other foods involves the use of the tongue and jaws.

Startling Blue Tongue

In the wild the main predators of the blue-tongued skink are large birds such as brown falcons and laughing kookaburras. Dingoes, monitor lizards, eastern brown snakes, red-bellied black snakes, and the Mulga snake also attack it. In suburban gardens dogs and cats are additional hazards. Unable to rely on speed to escape, the blue-tongued skink inflates its body, hisses loudly, and opens its mouth. At the same time, it thrusts out its broad, blue tongue that contrasts with the pinkish-red lining of its mouth, giving the impression that it is deadly.

If necessary, it will deliver a bite using its strong jaws. Because of this defensive behavior blue-tongued skinks were once thought to be venomous, and many were killed by humans.

Breeding Behavior

Male blue-tongued skinks have a longer, more slender body than the females. The difference is apparent in newborns and adults but harder to spot in partly grown specimens. The skinks tend

⊙ *The Centralian blue-tongued skink,* Tiliqua multifasciata, *is slightly smaller than* T. scincoides. *Its coloration enables it to remain concealed against the arid red sand of its native habitat in the Australian interior.*

to be solitary for the majority of the year. In most parts of their range they either hibernate or experience slightly cooler conditions for six to 12 weeks depending on temperatures. After emerging in spring (September to October), males become more active. They increase the size of their home range as they look for females. As in other species of skink, male-to-male encounters can result in combat and serious injury.

When meeting a receptive female, the male grips her neck or shoulder in his powerful jaws, aligns his body with hers, and scratches her back with a hind leg. With these movements she becomes passive and raises her tail to allow mating to take place. Mating lasts for two to four minutes. If the female is unreceptive, she may try to escape, causing serious damage to her neck or shoulder from the male's jaws. After mating, males often rub their cloaca along the ground—this behavior may be a form of scent marking. Observers have reported males guarding mated females for periods of up to 25 days after copulation.

Mated females spend more time basking, which increases their chances of predation. As the time of birth approaches, the size and number of young cause the female to rest with her hind legs and tail raised. The young are born approximately 110 days after mating. While developing, they have been nourished by a placentalike organ. During birth they rupture the embryonic membrane and consume the yolk sac and membrane before dispersing.

There is no parental care. The female eats any undeveloped ova that emerge at the same time. The number of young produced tends to increase with the female's size and age. Female fertility is low—in many parts of their range they may not breed every year, especially if there is a shortage of food. The young skinks reach adulthood at three years old.

Live-Bearing—the Pros and Cons

All species of blue-tongued skinks give birth to live young. This method of reproduction protects the young from some environmental hazards. In temperate areas the female blue-tongued skink is able to thermoregulate by choosing and maintaining positions with higher temperatures, thereby increasing her body temperature and that of the developing young. Eggs buried in the ground would not be able to reach the same temperature for long enough, and development would be halted. Because the young develop inside the female's body, they can feed and accumulate reserves before the onset of winter hibernation.

It is thought that viviparity (live-bearing) has evolved in blue-tongued skinks and other large species because the adults are less vulnerable to predation, which means that the young have a greater chance of survival. Another theory is that they do not depend on speed to escape from enemies or to obtain food, and females are not inconvenienced by the additional weight and bulk of the developing young. However, there are disadvantages. If the female blue-tongued skink is killed while gravid, all the young die too. Also, multiple clutches do not occur—in fact, most female blue-tongued skinks only breed every second year.

The young of Tiliqua scincoides are born live rather than hatching from an egg. These two are just five days old. Females reproduce every second year and can give birth to up to 25 young.

Common name Stump-tailed skink (*Boggi,* sleepy lizard, pine-cone lizard, bob-tailed lizard, shingleback lizard)

Scientific name *Trachydosaurus rugosus*

Family Scincidae

Suborder Sauria

Order Squamata

Size From 16 in (41 cm) to 18 in (46 cm)

Key features Heavy bodied with triangular-shaped head; ear openings conspicuous; legs noticeably reduced; toes short; tail blunt and short and resembles head; scales large, rough, knobby; tongue blue; body color and pattern vary with location, can be uniform dark brown or black or have contrasting bands or flecks of white, yellow, or gray

Habits Basks early in the day to raise temperature, followed by periods of feeding; retreats to shelter toward the end of the day

Breeding Live-bearer; female produces 1 or 2 young; gestation period 5 months

Diet Omnivorous; mainly plant and vegetable matter supplemented with insects, snails, and carrion

Habitat Semiarid plains and drier woodlands

Distribution Southern Australia from New South Wales to the coast of Western Australia; also Rottnest Island off the coast of Western Australia

Status Locally common

Similar species None

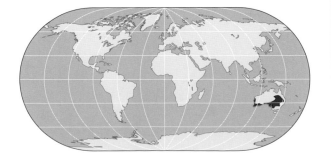

Stump-Tailed Skink
Trachydosaurus rugosus

Despite having to withstand extremes of temperature and even drought, the strange-looking stump-tailed skink is long-lived. It is common over much of southern and Western Australia.

STUMP-TAILED SKINK IS JUST ONE NAME used when referring to *Trachydosaurus rugosus*. Others include the Aboriginal *Boggi* (or "sleepy lizard" because of its slow-moving habits), the pine-cone lizard (from the shape of its scales), and the bob-tailed lizard (from the shape of its tail).

There is also some dispute over its exact taxonomic status. Initially it was placed in its own genus, *Trachydosaurus*. Some years later it was reclassified as *Tiliqua rugosa*, based on similarities to members of the genus *Tiliqua* (such as its blue tongue, omnivorous feeding habits, and the fact that it bears live young). In 1992 it was reassigned to the genus *Trachydosaurus* on the basis of the lack of lobes in front of the ear openings, scalation differences from members of the genus *Tiliqua*, and the fact that it has divided scales (lamellae) on the undersides of the toes on its hind feet.

It was given the name *Trachydosaurus rugosus*, and four subspecies were recognized: *Trachydosaurus rugosus rugosus*, the nominate form from Western Australia, *T. r. aspera* from eastern Australia, *T. r. konowi* from Rottnest Island off the coast of Western Australia, and *T. r. palarra* from the midwest coast.

Range of Habitats
Although the stump-tailed skink is widely distributed over the southern half of Australia, it is absent from the coastal fringes and mountain ranges of eastern and southeastern parts of the country and Tasmania. Present in Queensland, New South Wales, Victoria, South

⬆ **Head detail of the stump-tailed skink, showing the large, irregular scales and the small eye with its movable lower eyelid.**

Australia, and Western Australia, the species has a large range that encompasses a variety of microclimates. Habitat varies from dry forest, hummock grassland, woodland, to scrubland and desert. Stump-tailed skinks are more common in some areas than others, and population densities vary from 0.3 to 5.5 specimens per 2.5 acres (1 ha). In Western Australia the skinks are frequently seen in gardens, on farms, and crossing roads. It is traffic that is responsible for most adult stump-tailed skink fatalities. Within such varied habitats the stump-tailed skink experiences a wide range of climatic conditions. Generally speaking, summers are harsh and dry, winters are cool, and spring is wet. Temperatures in the more arid parts can exceed 129°F (53.5°C) on hot summer days and fall to 24°F (-5°C) on winter nights. Dust storms, sand storms, excessive droughts, and temporary floods present additional problems for

Opportunistic Omnivores

Stump-tailed skinks are omnivorous, and they feed opportunistically. Their diet consists mainly of fruit and vegetable matter, including native currant and blackthorn berries, fungi, herbs, grasses, and seedlings. They are particularly fond of flowers, especially yellow-colored ones, and will gorge on these blossoms in early summer. The rest of their diet includes insects, particularly grasshoppers, and carrion, the latter being an important food source when vegetation is scarce. As well as being partial to the eggs of ground-nesting birds and the young of mammals found in burrows, *Trachydosaurus rugosus* is fond of snails. It uses its powerful jaws to crush them before maneuvering its tongue to separate the mollusk from its shell, which it discards.

Such opportunistic feeding habits are key to the skink's survival. In many parts of its range it experiences periods of drought and famine. Food is abundant during the spring months after late winter rain, but supplies decrease during summer and fall, so the skink has to rely on fat stored in its bulbous tail. By the end of winter its tail may become very thin. The skink seems to have adapted by feeding well in spring and eating little during the rest of the year. It is diurnal and therefore most active during spring. It is not uncommon for the late winter rains to fail—in those areas spring food supplies are low, and the stump-tailed skink may have to survive for 15 months on comparatively little food, leading to a number of deaths the following fall and winter.

⊕ *An adult female stump-tailed skink lies close to her young in woodland in Western Australia.*

the skink. To escape the extreme temperatures, it takes refuge in rabbit warrens and the burrows of other animals, in leaf litter, and under rotten logs. Having a tough, thick skin keeps water loss to a minimum and helps it survive in arid areas. The tail is used to store fat—if necessary, the skink can go for several months without feeding.

A Pine Cone on Legs

The stump-tailed skink is one of the larger members of the family Scincidae and grows up to 18 inches (46 cm) long. Its triangular-shaped head has fragmented, irregular scales. Its eyes are comparatively small, and only the lower lid is movable. Ear openings are large and lack the anterior lobes characteristic of *Tiliqua* species.

The broad tongue is blue and contrasts with the pink lining of the mouth. The stout, elongated body is covered with large, overlapping scales that make it look a little like a pine cone. Legs in this species are

considerably reduced and have five short, fat digits. The most noticeable feature is its short, blunt tail, which resembles the head and is designed to confuse predators. Although the tail has a fracture plane and can therefore break off in order to allow the skink to escape, its loss could have serious consequences for the lizard, since one of its functions is as a valuable fat store when food is scarce.

Color and pattern variations follow geographic trends. Individuals from the interior of New South Wales tend to be uniform dark brown to black. In Renmark, southern Australia, stump-tailed skinks have a pattern of bright-yellow blotches on a background of chocolate-brown. Those inhabiting Western Australia are particularly attractive, being orange-brown with whitish dorsal crossbands. The subspecies *T. r. konowi* from Rottnest Island is considerably

Seasonal Monogamy

The peak mating time for stump-tailed skinks is October through early November. Differences between the sexes are slight: Males have a blunter head and a slightly longer, narrower tail than females. The skinks have a complex social structure in which pairs are monogamous during the breeding season. Although they separate for the winter, they pair up again during the next breeding season.

The pairs are also faithful over a number of years. This implies that there is long-term recognition of individuals. Usually the male attempts to relocate the female by following trails using airborne signals or by searching familiar sites. It is thought that the complex social structure is allowed to develop because the stump-tailed skinks are quite long-lived animals (20 or more years) and have a relatively low reproductive rate.

smaller at 10.5 inches (26 cm) long. It is dark brown with small white to gray flecks on the back and underside.

As well as the color differences there are also variations in the length and shape of the tail. Stump-tailed skinks from the east have shorter, fatter tails than those from the western part of the range. The skink's normal movements are slow and deliberate, but despite its short legs and bulky body, it can move quite fast at times.

Defensive Display

When confronted by a predator or a human enemy, the stump-tailed skink adopts a defensive posture. It curves its body into a semicircle and throws open its mouth to reveal the blue tongue and contrasting pink lining—this is known as threat coloration. At the same

Large Babies and Longevity

Producing small numbers of large young has an obvious benefit in terms of survival—there is less risk of predation on the newborn skinks. The larger birth size also enables the young to put on substantial growth during the spring of their birth, helping them withstand the drought and famine of the summer and fall. Notwithstanding, survival rates are low, with only 4 percent of newborns reaching adulthood, which can take between three and five years depending on food supply. Stump-tailed skinks have a long life span (about 20 years). This is unusual compared to many other skinks, which are short-lived and experience a rapid turnover. The disadvantage of the stump-tailed skinks' low reproductive rate is offset by their longevity, which sustains stable populations in the long run.

⤵ *In response to a threat the stump-tailed skink creates a defensive display involving curving its body and showing the bright colors inside its mouth.*

time, it hisses. The skink then circles to face its enemy; should the warnings fail and the predator come within reach, it snaps with its powerful jaws and delivers a painful bite with its sharp teeth.

Mating and Birth

During the mating season pairs of stump-tailed skinks can be seen together with either the male moving slowly closely followed by the female or the pair resting and frequently touching each other. They are not generally known for exhibiting aggressive behavior, but at this time males can show aggression to unattached younger males.

Once he has found a mate, the male grasps her neck or shoulders in his powerful jaws. In this way he is able to align their cloacae to allow mating to take place. Stump-tailed skinks are viviparous (live-bearing) and produce one or two young after a gestation period of four to four and a half months. A type of placenta forms between the female and the developing embryos, allowing the exchange of food and waste products to take place.

The young are born in late March to early April and may be almost half the size of the female. Research has shown that the female is capable of recognizing her own offspring using chemical cues for at least two months after she has given birth.

Common name Crocodile skink
(casque-headed skink)

Scientific name *Tribolonotus gracilis*

Family   Scincidae

Suborder   Sauria

Order   Squamata

Size   8 in (20 cm)

Key features Head triangular shaped with casque at rear; body scales large and spiny; scales on tail point backward; body color brown on the back with a yellowish-brown underside; orange ring surrounds most of the eye; yellow pigment present on anterior edge of the eye

Habits   Mainly active at dusk; semiburrower, spends much of the time in leaf litter or under foliage on banks of streams

Breeding   Egg layer; female lays 1 (occasionally 2) eggs that hatch after 65–75 days; several clutches laid in a season

Diet   Omnivorous

Habitat   Forest and coconut plantations close to water

Distribution New Guinea

Status   Vulnerable (IUCN)

Similar species *Tribolonotus novaeguineae*

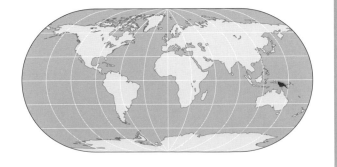

Crocodile Skink

Tribolonotus gracilis

The little-known crocodile skink was only discovered recently. The large, spiny scales from which it gets its common name look like armor plating and give it an almost prehistoric appearance.

THE CROCODILE SKINK occurs only in Irian Jaya and North Papua, New Guinea, and on Kar Kar Island off the coast of New Guinea. These slow-moving skinks are mainly active at dusk or at night. They inhabit wet, tropical forests and spend much of the day under rotting vegetation in shaded mountain valleys close to water. They often dig a series of tunnels in the soft soil. They are good swimmers and can remain totally immersed for at least 20 minutes.

Daytime temperatures in the region range from 73 to 82°F (23–28°C), falling to 68°F (20°C) at night. Humidity is from 80 to 90 percent. Crocodile skinks are relatively social lizards that live in small groups consisting of one male and one or more females. Such a social structure encourages parental care.

Armor Plating

The head of the skink is enlarged and triangular shaped. Six large scales at the nape of the neck give a casque- or helmetlike appearance from which it gets the alternative common name of casque-headed skink. Its few body scales are large and spiny (whereas those of other members of the genus are keeled). Four rows of raised scales run along the back to the tip of the tail. Glands associated with scent secretion and communication are located under the abdominal scales as well as on the surfaces of the hands and the undersides of the feet.

Its body color is mid- to dark brown on the back with a yellowish-brown underside. A striking feature is the orange ring surrounding all but the upper edge of the eye. At the front edge of the eye yellow pigment is also present.

⊖ *Bearing a strong resemblance to a mini crocodile,* Tribolonotus gracilis *is unusual among members of its genus in that its scales are large and spiny instead of keeled.*

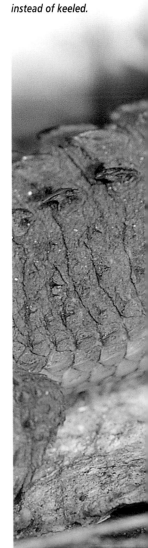

Vocal Skinks

Crocodile skinks feed on a variety of insects, beetles, millipedes, and centipedes. They grab their prey in their jaws and crush it before swallowing.

Crocodile skinks are egg layers. In the female the left oviduct and ovary are reduced, an unusual feature in reptiles. Because of their secretive nature little is known about the act of mating, but the female lays a single, large egg in leaf litter and curls around it. She guards it carefully, but the male shows no defensive behavior toward the egg. Some 65 to 75 days later the hatchling emerges. Soon afterward the female lays another egg. She can identify her hatchling, and maternal care continues for two or three weeks. During this time the youngster often climbs onto its mother's back. She will cry out at any sign of danger to the young. The male shows no interest in the young; nor does he display hostility toward them.

Although vocalization is known to exist among the geckos (family Gekkonidae) and the flap-footed lizards (family Pygopodidae), it was only in 2001 that evidence of vocalization in *Tribolonotus gracilis* was discovered. It appears that the sounds are produced by air as it is exhaled. Anatomical specializations within the larynx allow the skink to vary the pattern of the call, producing harmonics. Females are capable of producing a greater range, but the calls of males last longer than those of females. Larger males produce more high-frequency sounds, and this may indicate sexual dimorphism.

Vocalization is associated with defense. If attacked, the skink stands on extended legs with its tail raised and performs open-mouthed lunges at the source of the danger. This is accompanied by distress calls. Females also emit calls if there is a potential threat to their eggs or young.

Alligator and Glass Lizards

The family Anguidae contains 113 species of lizards divided among four subfamilies and 12 to 14 genera. They occur in North, Central, and South America, on some Caribbean islands, in North Africa, Europe, and Asia. They have a variety of shapes and lifestyles. Some species have small but perfectly formed limbs, some have rudimentary legs, and others have no legs at all. Most species are terrestrial, but there are also arboreal and burrowing species. Finally, some species lay eggs, but most are live-bearing. Live-bearers may simply retain their eggs in their bodies where the embryos are nourished by the yolk sac, or they may nourish the young directly through a primitive type of placenta.

Common Features

There is no one characteristic that sets anguids apart from other lizards, making them hard to describe in general terms, but they do share some common anatomical features. They are all heavily armored with thick scales that are often squarish in shape and arranged in distinct rows down their body. The scales have bony plates called osteoderms underneath them for extra protection, and it is these plates that make anguids rigid (compared to snakes, for instance, which are much more supple). Many species have a fold or pleat along their sides between the front and hind limbs (if they are present).

Their teeth are nearly solid, and new teeth come up behind the ones they are replacing, not under them as in most other lizards. Their jaws are powerful, and they can give a painful bite. Their tongue is divided into two parts. The front section is fixed in shape and size, but the back section is elastic. The front and back sections are separated by a fold, and the lizard can withdraw the front part inside the back part, which forms a sheath. The tip of the tongue is notched but not as deeply as in snakes. Anguids use their tongue in the same way as snakes do to explore their surroundings and constantly flick it in and out to examine objects.

Habitat

Anguids live in a wide range of habitats from deserts and sand dunes to grasslands and rain forests. The greatest concentration of species is in Central America and the West Indies, but several live in much colder parts. The slow worm, *Anguis fragilis*, for example, almost reaches the Arctic Circle in Scandinavia, while the northern alligator lizard, *Elgaria coerulea*, reaches farther north into Canada than any other American lizard.

The Anguidae is a versatile family whose members have moved into a number of different habitats, giving rise to a variety of body shapes that reflect their differing lifestyles. Burrowing species usually lack limbs, as do some terrestrial species that crawl through dense undergrowth. Terrestrial species from more open habitats have small but functional legs, and arboreal species have legs adapted for climbing. Some of the latter also have prehensile tails.

The Anguidae is divided into four subfamilies, each of which has a fairly distinct set of characteristics.

Common name Alligator and glass lizards **Family** Anguidae

Family Anguidae 4 subfamilies, 12 or 14 genera, 113 species of alligator and glass lizards

Subfamily Anguinae—2 genera, 16 species of legless lizards with a widespread distribution, including the slow worm, *Anguis fragilis*

Subfamily Diploglossinae—3 or 5 genera, 49 species from Central and South America, including the giant galliwasps, *Celestus* and *Diploglossus*

Subfamily Gerrhonotinae—6 genera, 46 species from North and Central America, including the North American alligator lizards, *Elgaria* and *Gerrhonotus*

Subfamily Anniellinae —1 genus (*Anniella*), 2 species of burrowing legless lizards from California and Baja California

---

SEE ALSO Lizards **44:**8; Slow Worm **46:**56; Lizard, Eastern Glass **46:**60; Lizard, European Glass **46:**62; Snakes **48:**8

⊕ *In Mexico* Barisia imbricata *(subfamily Gerrhonotlnae), sometimes known as the scorpion lizard, lives on the ground in conifer and oak forests.*

Subfamily Anguinae

Members of the subfamily Anguinae are all legless. The slow worm, *Anguis fragilis*, gives its name to the subfamily and the family, and is a well-known European species. The name *fragilis* refers to its tail, which is easily broken (although this applies equally to many other members of the family). Its common name, slow worm, is harder to explain because it is not particularly slow, and it certainly isn't a worm. It has a large range over much of Europe and Central Asia. The only other species in the genus, *A. cephallonica*, lives in southern Greece and was only recently recognized as distinct—it used to be a subspecies of the slow worm, *A. fragilis cephallonica*.

The genus *Ophisaurus* is represented in Europe by a single species, *O. apodus*, the European glass lizard, or scheltopusik. Its scientific name means "legless snake lizard." It is the largest member of the family and measures about 4.5 feet (1.4 m) including its long tail. It is a common grassland species.

The other glass lizards, all in the same genus, *Ophisaurus*, are from North America, India, and the Far East, with one species found in North Africa. The American species are familiar but secretive lizards that are found mostly on the eastern side of the United States. All these species can break off their tails easily if they are caught, hence the name "glass lizards."

Subfamily Diploglossinae

The Diploglossinae is a subfamily of mostly long, thin lizards with small limbs, although a small number of large species are heavier in build. Some species have a reduced number of toes on their limbs as a "halfway" stage toward losing them, and the *Ophiodes* species from South America have lost their front legs altogether, although they have very small back legs. These species live in grasslands and forest clearings. Members of the genera *Celestus* and *Diploglossus*, with 27 and 11 species respectively, live in the Caribbean region, in Central America, and on the West Indian islands. On the latter they occur mainly on the larger islands, such as Jamaica, Cuba, and Hispaniola, which all have several species.

Members of both genera resemble skinks with small, shiny scales covering their bodies and large, platelike shields on their heads. All the *Celestus* species are live-bearers, but *Diploglossus*, sometimes called galliwasps, contains egg-laying and live-bearing species. Some species are quite colorful: Juvenile *D. fasciatus* are boldly banded in black and white, for example. Males tend to be larger than females and are often more brightly colored. Two small genera, *Sauresia* and *Wetmorena*, with two and one species respectively, are sometimes included within *Diploglossus* and are very similar to them. They are confined to the West Indian island of Hispaniola.

Subfamily Gerrhonotinae

The third subfamily is the Gerrhonotinae. Its members have wide heads, powerful jaws, chunky bodies that are often almost square in cross-section, and well-developed legs. It contains the North American alligator lizards, *Elgaria* and *Gerrhonotus*, and four other genera from Central America. Alligator lizards are typical ground-dwelling species that live in habitats such as forest edges, hillsides, and semideserts. The other genera live in a wide range of habitats from rain forests to highland forests.

The *Abronia* species are climbers and have prehensile tails. They are sometimes found sheltering in bromeliads (air plants). These lizards do not have common names, although they are sometimes called dwarf alligator lizards. There are 26 named species in the genus, but scientists suspect there are several more awaiting description. They all have very restricted ranges in the highlands of Mexico and neighboring Central American countries, where they live in humid pine and oak forests. They are often cryptically colored to blend in with the lichen-covered branches among which they live, and as far as anyone knows, they are all live-bearers. Litter size of the known species is small, usually five or six, although it may be up to 12 in one species, *A. vasconcelosi*. Sadly, the *Abronia* species are disappearing along with the forests in which they live. Because they live in such small pockets of suitable habitat, they are especially vulnerable to forest clearance and development for agriculture. Conservationists expect at least one-third of all species to disappear in the near future.

Two other genera in the subfamily are the North American alligator lizards, *Elgaria* (seven species) and *Gerrhonotus* (two species). *Gerrhonotus liocephalus* and *G. lugoi* are both egg layers and are from the southern United States and Mexico respectively. *Elgaria* contains both live-bearing and egg-laying species. Alligator lizards are handsome, adaptable lizards that occupy a range of different habitats, including areas that have been altered by human activities.

All four *Barisia* species come from Mexico. They are very similar to the North American alligator lizards and are all live-bearers. The same applies to the six *Mesaspis* species that range from Mexico to Panama and live in montane habitats. *Coloptychon rhombifer* from lowland forests of Costa Rica and northwestern Panama is the only member of its genus and is rare and poorly known. Superficially it looks like an elongated alligator lizard. Its method of reproduction is unknown.

⊕ *Alligator lizards in the genus* Abronia *often shelter in bromeliad plants and can be cryptically colored to blend in with the general background colors of the Central American forests where they live.*

Subfamily Anniellinae

The subfamily Anniellinae is sometimes placed in a family of its own, the Anniellidae. There are only two species, *Anniella pulchra* and *A. geronomensis*, both of which are small, burrowing, legless lizards from the coasts of California and Baja California. They live just beneath the surface in sand dunes, sandy soil, and leaf litter. They both give birth to live young.

Ancient Origins

The anguids are among the more advanced lizards. Along with the monitors in the family Varanidae, the beaded lizards in the family Helodermatidae, and the Borneo earless monitor, *Lanthanotus borneensis*, they belong to a branch of reptiles called the anguinomorphs whose ancestry can be traced back to some of the most spectacular lizards that have ever lived—the huge marine mososaurs. These awesome predators, some growing up to 40 feet (12 m) long, first appeared in the Cretaceous Period about 120 million years ago. But they were short-lived and disappeared during the "mass extinction" of reptiles at the end of that period. Of the surviving lizards the anguids are most closely related to the Xenosauridae, a small and poorly known family whose members live in Central America and southeast China.

Carnivorous Hunters

All members of the Anguidae are carnivorous, although some of the larger galliwasps may eat plant material as well. They will tackle most types of prey, and the diets of the various species are probably based more on their size and what is available than on any particular preferences. Since most of them are small to medium sized, the prey that will be most readily available to them will be insects and spiders. Some species, such as the slow worm, eat large quantities of slugs, and the larger ones also eat snails.

A few species are big enough to tackle small rodents and other vertebrates, including other lizards. Alligator lizards sometimes climb into bushes and raid birds' nests. They have powerful jaws that they use to pin down and crush their prey. Although most of them ignore food that is not alive and moving, the large European glass lizard is more than happy to eat pieces of meat in captivity and probably eats carrion in the wild. Some alligator lizards also eat carrion.

Methods of hunting are straightforward in all the species that have been studied. They seem to hunt mainly by smell. Most of the temperate species are active in the day, and they nose about among dead leaves, tussocks of grass, and under trash. As they move methodically over the area, they push their snouts into nooks and crannies,

Long Body or Long Tail?

All the legless species of anguids are elongated. However, there is a strong correlation between lifestyle and the way in which they are elongated. Burrowing species such as the California legless lizards, *Anniella*, have an elongated body and short tail, giving them proportions similar to those of burrowing snakes. They use their body to drive themselves through loose soil or sand in a swimming type of motion.

Surface-dwelling legless species, however, such as the glass lizards, *Ophisaurus*, have an elongated tail and short body. When these species move, it is mainly the tail that pushes against the ground. This "rule" applies to legless lizards in general, not just anguids. Therefore, faced with a legless lizard, it should be possible to predict its lifestyle without knowing which species it is or even to which family it belongs simply by looking at its body shape and tail size. Species that live on the ground in forest, scrub, or semidesert situations and that have very reduced legs are all long-tailed forms.

⊜ *Ophiodes species lizards (subfamily Diploglossinae) lack front legs and have tiny back legs. They live in grassland and forest clearings. This is* O. yacupoi *from southwestern Brazil.*

using their notched tongue to identify a possible meal, continuously "tasting" the air and the ground. On the other hand, their eyes are small, and they have trouble seeing stationary objects. Anything that moves is likely to be grabbed in their jaws with a quick, darting movement. Feeding methods in tropical species are virtually unknown.

Reproduction Methods

Some anguid lizards lay eggs, while others give birth to live young. Some of those that lay eggs coil around them and guard them until they hatch. The North American and European species all mate in the spring in April, May,

or early June depending on the weather and conditions. Egg-laying species produce their clutches about one to two months later, and species that live in warmer parts, such as California, may go on to lay a second or even a third clutch in the same year.

Numbers of eggs can vary from five to 20 per clutch. The length of time the eggs take to hatch depends on species but is typically just over one month. Live-bearing species have a long gestation period and only have time to produce one clutch each year. Not much is known about the breeding habits of the tropical species. Most of them are live-bearing, but there are both live-bearing and egg-laying species among the *Diploglossus* species.

Common name Slow
worm (blind worm)

Scientific name *Anguis fragilis*

Subfamily Anguinae

Family Anguidae

Suborder Sauria

Order Squamata

Size Up to 20 in (51 cm) but usually shorter

Key features Legless lizard; scales smooth and shiny;
head no wider than its body; no distinct neck
region; eyes small; tail longer than body
when complete; color brown, sometimes
coppery; females have a thin dark line down
the center of the back and dark flanks; males
usually uniform in color; juveniles look like
females but are often more brightly colored

Habits Terrestrial; semiburrowing; active at night;
occasionally basks in the day

Breeding Live-bearer; female gives birth to 6–12 young;
gestation period 8–12 weeks

Diet Soft-bodied invertebrates, especially small
slugs, snails, and worms; insects and small
lizards

Habitat Damp places with plenty of vegetation,
including woodland clearings, hedges, banks,
gardens, parks, and railway embankments

Distribution Most of Europe except the southern half of
Spain and the most northerly parts of
Scandinavia; east Asia to west Siberia, the
Caucasus, northern Turkey, northwest Iran

Status Common

Similar species Young European glass lizards, *Ophisaurus
apodus*, but they are spotted; snakes are
more supple, lack eyelids, and have a single
row of wide scales down the belly

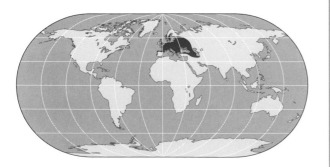

Slow Worm

Anguis fragilis

*Sometimes mistaken for a snake,
the slow worm is, in fact, a legless
lizard. It is often found in gardens
across Europe and is the
gardener's friend, since it feeds
on many invertebrate pests.*

THE SLOW WORM IS OFTEN MISTAKEN for a snake, but
even a superficial examination reveals that its
movements are less agile, its eyelids are
movable, and it has a short, notched tongue—
all of which distinguish it from a snake. Also, as
in other legless lizards, its tongue can only be
extended when it opens its mouth slightly,
while snakes protrude their tongue through a
small notch in the lower jaw (the lingual fossa).

The slow worm's underside is covered by
several rows of scales, with each scale being
roughly the same shape as those on its back.
(This also differentiates it from snakes, which
have a single row of specialized scales along
their underside.) When a slow worm is picked

Spot the Difference

For a species with such a huge geographical range slow worms
show surprisingly little variation. The population in the southern
Peloponnese and the Ionian Islands, Greece, is more slender and has
a proportionately longer tail, but it has now been reclassified as a
separate species, *Anguis cephallonica*. In eastern Europe the
subspecies *A. fragilis colchicus* has more rows of scales around its
body on average, and males often have blue spots along the sides of
their body, especially around the head and neck. Western individuals
belonging to the nominate subspecies also have these spots
sometimes, and the two forms are impossible to tell apart without
information relating to locality. Other than these slight variations slow
worms from northern Scotland look much the same as slow worms
from Scandinavia, western Siberia, or the Balkans.

up, it may try to coil around your fingers but its body is neither as muscular nor as supple as a snake's, and it is unable to squeeze as tightly. Even so, many slow worms are killed needlessly in the belief that they are snakes.

Slow worms are secretive reptiles, rarely venturing out into the open except at night and then most commonly if it is damp, when their preferred prey—small gray slugs—are most active. They also eat snails, which they have to extract from their shells, and earthworms. These three items make up about 70 percent of their diet—the rest consists of insects and spiders. Slow worms also eat small vertebrates, including common and wall lizards, but they can only catch them on very rare occasions.

Slow worms are methodical feeders. They examine potential prey carefully by tongue-flicking. Then they raise the head slightly and make a short, deliberate, downward strike. If the prey moves, the process may be cut short, and the slow worm may react more quickly. After eating slugs or snails, it often wipes its jaws on moss or leaves to get rid of any slime.

Damp Habitats

Despite their wide range, slow worms' habitats tend to have several things in common. They prefer slightly damp habitats with plenty of ground cover in the form of grasses and low-growing vegetation. In agricultural regions they are often concentrated at the bottom of hedges and odd pieces of ground at the edges and corners of fields that get missed by the plow, although these places are becoming rarer. They also live on commons, "waste" land, and rough grazing, and are sometimes found in overgrown parks, gardens, and cemeteries. Railway cuttings and embankments are often rich in slow worms, which thrive on the sunny, south-facing slopes. These "dispersal corridors" often reach into the hearts of cities, and slow worms take advantage by spreading into adjacent gardens and vegetable plots.

⊕ *Like many reptiles, slow worms use their notched tongue to find prey, flicking it in and out of the mouth to pick up scent particles in the air.*

57

Slow worms rarely come onto the surface during the day. They prefer to stay under cover in disused rodent burrows or under objects lying on the surface. In suitable habitats one or more slow worms are likely to be found under flat rocks, slates, old sacking, carpets, or concrete slabs, basking in the heat that penetrates there. Because these places are also damp, they often act as magnets for slugs and snails as well, which makes them even more attractive to the slow worms. Slow worms will burrow through loose soil and leaf litter if necessary; but since they have no adaptations for burrowing, they nearly always use ready-made tunnels and underground chambers.

Fragile Tails

The slow worm's generic name *Anguis* means snake, showing that even the most famous zoologist of all, the "Father of Taxonomy," Carl Linnaeus, got it wrong some of the time. Its specific name, *fragilis*, is more accurate and stems from the lizard's tendency to lose its tail in response to an attack by a predator. In many populations nearly all adults have stumpy or regrown tails, often as a result of attacks by domestic cats. However, since they resemble worms, they have many enemies, including birds of prey, magpies and crows, domestic chickens, snakes, weasels, small boys, and other predatory mammals.

Although they have powerful jaws they rarely bite, and their best means of defense is to let the predator have just their tail. Because their tail is so long, this strategy works more often than it might in other lizards. Statistically, the slow worm has about a 65 percent chance that any attack will be directed at its tail. And unlike other lizards, the slow worm seems not to be unduly hampered by losing its tail (unless it is attacked again before a new one grows). In studies on female slow worms scientists found that those with damaged tails gave birth to roughly the same number of young as those with complete tails, indicating that the tail is not essential for accumulating food that can be used later in the reproductive effort.

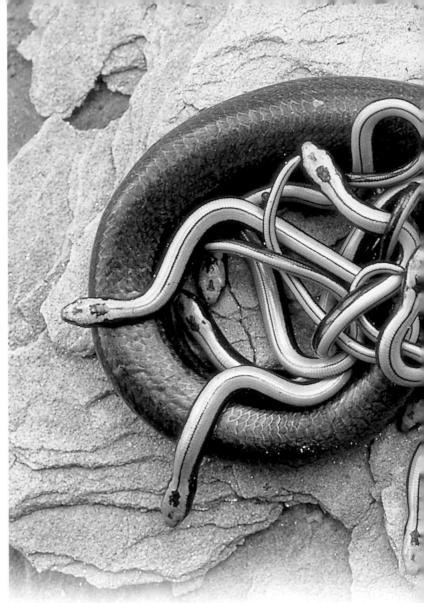

Slow worms will bask in the open just after emerging from hibernation in the spring or, in the case of females, just before they give birth in the late summer. At these times they may aggregate, and several can sometimes be found in the same spot. Five pregnant females were once found basking on the flat top of a stump partially covered with a thin sheet of moss in a place where they had never been seen before (and where they have never been seen since). Because they tend to appear and disappear intermittently in this way throughout the year, it is difficult to know whether slow worms are common (or even present) in an area. There have been few thorough studies on them, but some ecologists estimate that in particularly favorable habitats there may be as many as 250 to 800 individuals per 1 acre (0.4 ha).

Winter is spent deep underground, often in rodent burrows, where the slow worms are

⬆ Newborn slow worms are relatively small—2.8 to 4 inches (7–10 cm) long. The dorsal color is lighter than in the adults, usually a pale golden-brown or grayish silver, but their sides and underside are pitch black.

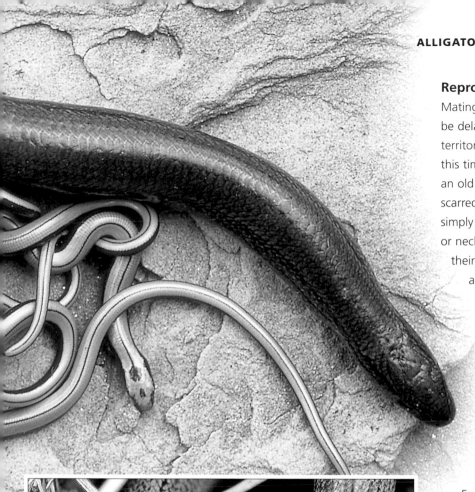

Reproduction

Mating usually takes place in May, but it may be delayed until the end of June. Males are not territorial, but they will fight off other males at this time of the year by biting—it is rare to find an old male slow worm that is not battle scarred. Courtship is not very subtle: The male simply pins down the female by biting her head or neck, twists his tail around hers, and aligns their cloacae. Mating can last up to 10 hours, and females may mate with more than one male in a season.

Most females do not breed every year, however, but in alternate years. In the Netherlands about 70 percent of females "rest" in dry years, whereas up to 90 percent may become pregnant in years with high rainfall (when there is plenty of food). These figures probably vary across the species' extensive range. Females continue to feed throughout their pregnancy, so they have a chance to breed two years in succession if conditions are good.

Females give birth from mid-August to October (or early November if gestation becomes drawn out during a cold summer). On rare occasions the female may not have given birth by the time she has to enter hibernation, and the young are born the following spring. Litter sizes vary greatly from three to 26, but most litters contain six to 12 young with an average of eight. As in other reptiles, larger females produce more young than smaller ones.

Young slow worms are born inside a membrane from which they escape by wriggling violently. They measure about 3 to 4 inches (7.6–10 cm) long and are a bright copper color. They double in length during their first year if all goes well. Males reach sexual maturity at about three years, females in five or six years, and they reach full adult size by the time they are about six to eight years old. Slow worms are very long-lived with an estimated life span of 10 to 12 years in the wild. In captivity, however, they can live much longer, with the record standing at 54 years.

⬆ *Courtship in slow worms is minimal, but mating takes up to 10 hours. This mating pair was photographed in the south of England.*

unharmed by frost. In northern Europe they do not emerge until March or even later, but in other parts of their range they may be active earlier than that depending on the climate.

They are most active near the surface between May and September, especially on warm days and during nights with light rain. Their preferred body temperature is 82°F (28°C), but they are active at temperatures as low as 58°F (14.5°C). If the temperature rises above 86°F (30°C), they retreat deeper underground until it becomes cooler.

Common name Eastern glass
lizard (Florida glass lizard)

Scientific name *Ophisaurus ventralis*

Subfamily Anguinae

Family Anguidae

Suborder Sauria

Order Squamata

Size 39 in (99 cm)

Key features A stiff, legless lizard with eyelids and
external ear openings; a groove along its side
marks the change from grayish-brown flanks
with white bars to the plain, off-white
underside; the back is plain brown in color;
side of the head is marked with dark-edged,
whitish bars, but they may disappear
with age

Habits Diurnal; terrestrial

Breeding Female lays 8–17 eggs that hatch after 8–9
weeks

Diet Invertebrates, especially slugs, snails, and
earthworms

Habitat Grassland, open woods, fields, and parks

Distribution Southeastern United Sates (North Carolina,
the whole of Florida, eastern Louisiana)

Status Common

Similar species The ranges of 3 other glass lizards—
the slender, the island, and the mimic
(*Ophisaurus attenuatus*, *O. compressus*, and
O. mimicus)—overlap the range of the
eastern glass lizard; the first 2 usually have
some black striping along their back or
flanks, while the mimic glass lizard is much
smaller, about 15 in (38 cm)

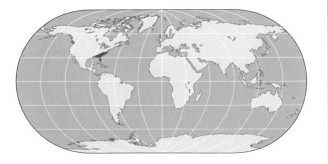

Eastern Glass Lizard
Ophisaurus ventralis

Glass lizards are well named: If their tail is held or attacked, it can shatter into several pieces, each of which continues to move independently.

GLASS LIZARDS SHOULD BE EASY TO DISTINGUISH from snakes because they have movable eyelids and external ear openings, whereas snakes do not. The head and body are only half as long as the tail (showing that it is a terrestrial rather than a burrowing species), while a snake's tail is generally about one-fifth of its total length. Glass lizards also have a distinct groove along each side of the body that allows it to expand when the lizard is distended with food or eggs.

A characteristic shared by all four North American glass lizards is the ability to lose and regrow the tail. A new, shorter tail will grow in its place, and adults with complete and original tails are rare. (The tail of the island glass lizard, *O. compressus*, does not have fracture planes like the other three species, and its tail is therefore not shed as easily.) The only other means of defense for glass lizards is to wriggle furiously and empty the contents of their cloacal glands, smearing and spraying them over their enemy.

Eastern glass lizards are usually found sheltering under objects lying on the ground, often pieces of board, tin, old carpet, or sacking. They are active during the day, especially early in the morning when the humidity is high, and their prey—slugs, snails, and earthworms—are most easily found.

Guarding the Eggs

Eastern glass lizards usually mate in the spring and lay eight to 17 eggs in May, June, or July. The eggs are laid in hollows in the ground, often under a log or flat rock. The female

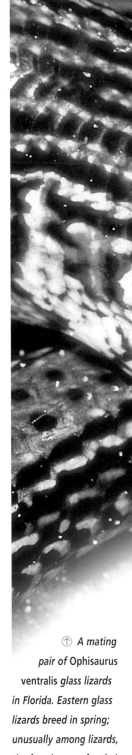

⊕ *A mating pair of* Ophisaurus ventralis *glass lizards in Florida. Eastern glass lizards breed in spring; unusually among lizards, the females care for their eggs by coiling around them until they hatch.*

Lateral Folds

All the glass lizards and many other members of the family (except the legless lizards, *Anniella*, and the slow worm, *Anguis fragilis*) have folds of skin along the sides of the body from the front legs to the back legs. The folded area is covered with small, soft scales, making it very flexible. The lizards need the fold because they have osteoderms (small bones) under their other scales. The bones make them so stiff that without the fold the lizards would not be able to expand their body to breathe, to take in large meals, or in the case of females, to hold developing eggs or young.

remains coiled around the eggs to guard them until they hatch during August and September.

Egg brooding in lizards is very rare. The only other species in which females are known to brood their eggs are the oviparous (egg-laying) members of the skink genus *Eumeces,* such as the prairie skink, *E. septentrionalis*, and the five-lined skink, *E. fasciatus*. Coincidentally, several of these species live in the same region as the glass lizards. The other members of the genus are viviparous (live-bearers). Some authorities think that egg brooding is the first evolutionary step toward viviparity.

Rare Relative

The mimic glass lizard, *O. mimicus*, was described to science only in 1987. It is the smallest glass lizard in North America, rarely exceeding 15 inches (38 cm) in total length, and is light tan to golden brown in color with several stripes. It is found in pine grasslands of northern Florida, coastal North Carolina, Georgia, and Mississippi.

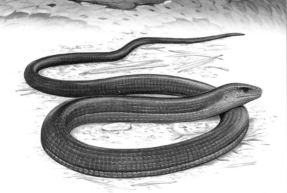

Common name European glass lizard (Pallas's glass lizard, scheltopusik)

Scientific name *Ophisaurus apodus*

Subfamily Anguinae

Family Anguidae

Suborder Sauria

Order Squamata

Size Up to 4.6 ft (1.4 m)

Key features Effectively legless, although reduced legs are present in the form of small, flipperlike flaps of skin on either side of the cloaca; body thick; tail accounts for about two-thirds of the total length; it has eyelids and small external ear openings; scales arranged in regular rows across and down the body; a fold of skin runs along the sides; color uniform brown, paler on the underside; juveniles are gray with irregular brown blotches and crossbars

Habits Terrestrial; diurnal

Breeding Female lays 6–10 eggs that hatch after 45–55 days

Diet Mostly invertebrates, especially snails, and occasional small vertebrates such as mice

Habitat Dry, rocky hillsides, sparse woodlands, fields, and meadows

Distribution Southeast Europe, the Caucasus, and part of the Crimean Peninsula

Status Very common in suitable habitat

Similar species Unlikely to be confused with any other reptile in the region

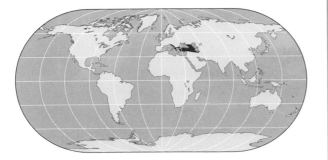

European Glass Lizard

Ophisaurus apodus

The European glass lizard is usually found in fairly dry habitats, often on rocky hillsides with some cover. It can sometimes be found sunning itself in meadows.

THE EUROPEAN GLASS LIZARD was first recognized as a legless lizard rather than a snake as long ago as 1775, when it was named *Lacerta apodus* by the German zoologist Peter Pallas. It is the largest legless lizard in the world, and is not only long but also stocky. Its body can be as thick as a human wrist.

Foul-Smelling Fluid

Adults can give a powerful bite if they are restrained, but they are normally harmless. When captured, their first line of defense is to defecate copiously over their captor. At the same time, they twist, spin, and hiss, ensuring that the obnoxious fluid is well distributed. If this does not have the desired effect (it usually does!), they may cause their tail to break off. But this is a last resort, and they are more reluctant than the American glass lizards to do this. They can regenerate a new tail if the old one is lost, but it does not grow back very well and is little more than a stump. Like the slow worm, *Anguis fragilis*, the European glass lizard has a short body and a proportionately long tail suited to its terrestrial (as opposed to burrowing) lifestyle.

It is an active species and is often quite conspicuous. In places where the grass is kept short by grazing animals, for example, individual glass lizards can even be seen from a passing car, lying stretched out in the turf. They usually remain still when they are first approached by a human but make off rapidly when the intruder reaches a distance of about 6 feet (1.8 m) away.

When foraging, they move slowly by lateral undulation and raise their head slightly from time to time, looking for possible food. They

⬇ *The most obvious feature of the European glass lizard is its apparent lack of limbs, but there are two very small stumps on either side of the cloaca. It also has the lateral fold along its body that is distinctive of many anguid species.*

also crawl up into the lower branches of bushes in this way. They may "paddle" their reduced hind limbs ineffectually when creeping slowly forward. When they hunt, they approach slow-moving prey such as snails with a rush; more agile prey (such as a grasshopper) is stalked more carefully—the lizard edges forward every time the grasshopper moves or is distracted.

Breeding

European glass lizards breed in the spring, usually from March to April. Nothing is known of their courtship. The female lays six to 12 eggs in an underground chamber (usually under a flat rock) about 10 weeks after mating and typically coils around them. She will chase off small animals that try to approach the nest. Egg guarding seems widespread in *Ophisaurus* and is practiced by all five species whose reproductive habits are known. The eggs hatch after 45 to 55 days, and the young glass lizards are about 4 to 5 inches (10–13 cm) long. They

are gray with wavy dark-brown crossbands, most of which end at the lateral fold, and their scales are more strongly keeled than those of the adults. They grow slowly, taking over four years to reach sexual maturity. When they shed their skin, it comes away piecemeal in rings. Some scientists report that related species, such as the North African glass lizard, *O. koellikeri*, only shed their skin very rarely with gaps of up to two years between each shedding.

Common Names

The alternative common names for the European glass lizard are Pallas's glass lizard and scheltopusik. Peter Pallas was a German zoologist who became a professor at St. Petersburg University in Russia. He first described and named the species in 1775. Scheltopusik also has Russian connections: It comes from the Russian word *zheltopuzik*, which means "yellow belly."

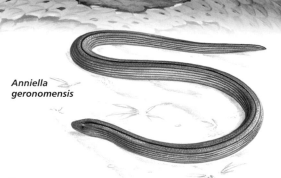

Anniella geronomensis

Common names
Baja California legless lizard (*A. geronomensis*); California legless lizard (*A. pulchra*)

Scientific names *Anniella geronomensis* and *A. pulchra*

Subfamily Anniellinae

Family Anguidae

Suborder Sauria

Order Squamata

Size From 6 in (15 cm) to 7 in (18 cm)

Key features Small legless lizards with few distinguishing marks; head small and pointed (when seen from the side) and not distinct from the neck; lower jaw deeply countersunk; eyes also sunk within the head and reduced to narrow horizontal slits; *A. geronomensis* is coppery or silvery brown in color with 7 or 8 thin black stripes running the length of the body; *A. pulchra* is similar but has 1 black line along the center of its back, another along each flank, and its underside is yellow

Habits Burrowers; sometimes bask on dunes but avoid extreme temperatures by moving around

Breeding Poorly known; may give birth to one or two live young in late summer or early fall

Diet Small invertebrates

Habitat Sand dunes (*A. geronomensis*) and sandy soils (*A. pulchra*)

Distribution Baja California, Mexico (*A. geronomensis*), southern California (*A. pulchra*)

Status Probably common in suitable habitat but localized and hard to find

Similar species None in the region

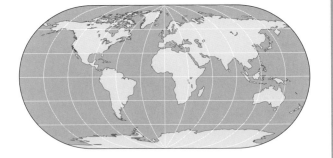

North American Legless Lizards

Anniella geronomensis and *A. pulchra*

Although common in some areas of their range, the North American legless lizards are considered species of special concern locally, and collecting them is restricted by law.

THE LITTLE NORTH AMERICAN legless lizards look superficially like young glass lizards, *Ophisaurus* species, or European slow worms, *Anguis fragilis*, but they are far more specialized. They spend most of their lives below the ground. Because they are burrowing species, they have long bodies and short tails (unlike all the other legless anguids, which have short bodies and long tails).

Sand Specialists

The Baja California species lives in the loose, windblown sand that forms a dune system stretching for about 54 miles (87 km) along the coast in the northern half of the peninsula. They are found nowhere else. They live among the roots of shrubs that grow on the dunes and travel between them by "swimming" through the sand just below the surface, leaving characteristic winding tracks. Early in the morning when the weather is cool, the lizards stay buried deep in the sand but come closer to the surface as soon as the sun begins to warm up the dunes.

Because the dunes are aligned north-south, the seaward, west-facing sides become very cool in the afternoon when the sun moves lower in the sky and the onshore breezes bring cold air. The inland side, however, does not benefit from the breezes, and the sun heats this side of the dunes up to temperatures that are dangerously high for the lizards. It seems that the lizards avoid the extremes of heat and cold by moving around to find the optimum

⌃ *California legless lizards, Anniella pulchra, are often seen among leaf litter and commonly burrow in soil near the surface. They differ from A. geronomensis in having three black lines along the body (rather than seven or eight) and a yellow underside.*

temperature. By late afternoon they often emerge to bask on the tops of the dunes where there is a fine balance between the heat of the sun and the cool breezes. They may stay on the surface to forage for food in the early part of the night before they become too cold. They also feed in the sand on burrowing insects and their larvae and small scorpions.

Farther north the California legless lizard is not so specialized. It lives on sandy and loamy soils, and can be found under stones and dead wood. It occurs on beaches, under debris, and among shrubs but in more compacted sand than the dunes farther south. In parts of California it is common in loose soil under juniper trees, where dead leaves provide an ideal habitat for the termites on which it feeds.

This species sometimes comes up toward the surface in the morning to bask under a flat rock or in the upper layer of soil and then emerges to hunt small insects and spiders. Where both species occur together, the Baja California species is the most common, but the California legless lizard can live farther inland

because it is not as strongly associated with loose sand as its coastal counterpart.

The Baja California species is inactive in midwinter, but the more northerly California legless lizard is active throughout the year. That is because the habitats along the Baja coast are more susceptible to the cooling effects of the Humboldt current, which brings cold fogs in from the sea. They burn off by the time they are a few miles inland, and the climate behind the fog zone is also far warmer in winter.

Little is known about the breeding habits of either species. Observations are based on a few captured specimens, making it hard to draw any firm conclusions. Female Baja California legless lizards have been found containing single embryos late in the year. Juveniles have been found in the spring and summer. This suggests that they mate in the spring and give birth late in the year. Similarly, the California legless lizard appears to give birth in late summer or early fall, and females of this species have been found with two embryos inside them.

Diploglossus monotropis

Common name Giant galliwasps

Scientific names *Celestus* sp. and *Diploglossus* sp.

Subfamily Diploglossinae

Family Anguidae

Suborder Sauria

Order Squamata

Size Body length over 12 in (30 cm); up to 18 in (46 cm) including tail

Key features Bulky, skinklike lizards with thick bodies, short limbs, and pointed snouts; heads covered with large, platelike scales; body scales shiny and overlapping with a rounded edge (cycloid); they have parallel ridges running down them (striations) that are better defined on some species than others; coloration varies, but most are shades of brown with orange or yellow markings; male *D. monotropis* are brightly marked in orange and yellow

Habits Diurnal or nocturnal depending on species; ground dwellers or semiburrowers

Breeding *Celestus sp.* are live-bearers; *Diploglossus* sp. may be live-bearers or egg layers; related species of egg-laying *Diploglossus* apparently coil around their incubating eggs

Diet Poorly known; large species are thought to be partly herbivorous; *C. occiduus* is reported to eat fish

Habitat Rain forests (among leaf litter) and swamps

Distribution Central America (*D. monotropis*) and the West Indies (Jamaica and Hispaniola)

Status Extremely rare, some possibly extinct

Similar species None in the region

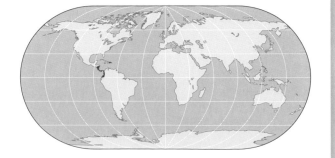

Giant Galliwasps

Celestus and *Diploglossus* sp.

Giant galliwasps form a very special group of six rare species. Some of them are threatened with imminent extinction.

THE GENERA *CELESTUS* AND *DIPLOGLOSSUS* contain 28 and 11 species respectively. Most are small to moderate in size. However, four species of *Celestus* (the Jamaican galliwasp, *C. occiduus*, the Haitian galliwasp, *C. warreni*, and two species from the Dominican Republic, *C. anelpistus* and *C. carraui*) and two species of *Diploglossus* (*D. monotropis* from Central America and *D. millepunctatus* from a tiny island off Colombia) are much larger with combined head and body lengths of over 8 inches (20 cm). They are known collectively as giant galliwasps, and the largest species is the one from Jamaica with a combined head and body length of over 12 inches (30 cm).

Endangered or Extinct

The only giant galliwasp that is not endangered is the Central American species, *D. monotropis*, which is rarely seen but widespread. The Jamaican galliwasp, *C. occiduus*, has not been seen since 1840, and many scientists think it is already extinct. However, it lives a secretive life in remote parts of the island, and a small population may have escaped notice. The Dominican species, *C. anelpistus*, lives (or lived) only in a small forest that was being destroyed even as the only four known specimens were collected in 1977. *Diploglossus millepunctatus* lives exclusively on the barren Malpelo Island west of Colombia. The other two species are rare but not critically endangered at present.

The main reasons for the decline of the giant galliwasps are habitat destruction resulting from land clearance for agricultural planting and the introduction of predators such as cats. A further pressure is that of wanton

⊕ *In Costa Rica a female galliwasp lizard, Diploglossus bilobatus, guards her clutch of eggs. Captive breeding programs involving similar, less rare members of the genus may ensure the future survival of the critically endangered species.*

Disappearing Giants

Reptiles that evolve on islands often exhibit gigantism (they are significantly larger than their relatives on the mainland). They have another, less welcome characteristic: They are more likely to go extinct because it takes less to upset the ecological balance on islands. Among the other giant island lizards that have disappeared in historical times are the Martinique giant ameiva, *Ameiva major* (Teiidae); the Cape Verde giant skink, *Macroscincus coctei* (Scincidae); and the Rodrigues giant day gecko, *Phelsuma gigas* (Gekkonidae).

Both species of giant tortoise, *Geochelone nigra* from the Galápagos Islands and *Dipsochelys dussumieri* from Aldabra, have been close to extinction, while others from Indian Ocean islands have disappeared in more recent times. In 1997 the last 12 Seychelles giant tortoises, *Dipsochelys hololissa*, were discovered in captivity on the islands and have been the subject of captive breeding programs in zoos throughout the world.

killing by indigenous people who often fear galliwasps and assume that they are venomous.

Galliwasps are the subject of several myths: People in Jamaica used to think that if you were bitten by a galliwasp and the galliwasp reached water first, you would die; but if you reached water first, the galliwasp would die. In parts of Panama and Costa Rica *D. monotropis* is called *el escorpion coral,* or the "coral snake lizard," because it is colored like a coral snake. Other variations include *la madre de coral*, "the

mother of coral snakes." In Haiti galliwasps are associated with voodoo superstitions and are often found hacked into pieces.

Experiment in Captive Breeding

The last hope for many of the giant galliwasps is to establish a captive breeding program to boost their numbers before releasing them into a secure habitat. Because they are so rare, the first step has been to set up breeding colonies of *C. warreni* (a more common species from Hispaniola) at Nashville Zoo in order to develop the necessary technique. It has proved very successful—over 300 offspring have been produced from nine pairs of lizards collected from the wild. The next step will be to use the knowledge gained to breed another large species, *D. monotropis*, before working with the critically endangered species.

It is also hoped that educational programs in places where the giant galliwasps occur naturally will lead to a better understanding of them and may help find previously unknown populations of the Jamaican galliwasp.

Common name
Southern alligator lizard

Scientific name *Elgaria multicarinata*

Subfamily Gerrhonotinae

Family Anguidae

Suborder Sauria

Order Squamata

Size From 10 in (25 cm) to 16 in (41 cm)

Key features A large lizard with a wide, triangular head
covered with large scales; forelimbs small;
hind limbs slightly larger; a fold runs along
each flank between the fore- and hind limbs;
scales on its back and flanks are roughly
square and keeled, giving it a ridged
appearance; color reddish brown or tan on
the back fading to grayish on the flanks,
usually with irregular black bands

Habits Diurnal; semiarboreal

Breeding Female lays 2–3 clutches of eggs each year

Diet Insects and spiders; occasional small lizards,
nestling birds and mice; also eats carrion

Habitat Moist grasslands and woodlands, especially in
foothills

Distribution Western North America (southern
Washington State south to Baja California
along a fairly narrow coastal belt)

Status Common

Similar species Several other alligator lizards live in the
same region; the northern alligator lizard,
Elgaria coerulea, is slightly smaller and has a
more speckled pattern

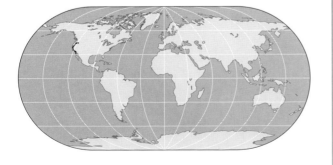

Southern Alligator Lizard

Elgaria multicarinata

Alligator lizards are so-called because they look like tiny alligators. They can also swim well and have a strong bite. Sometimes they even bite and then twist their entire body, like their larger namesakes.

THE SOUTHERN ALLIGATOR LIZARD is very much a generalist, occupying a range of different habitats and eating a wide variety of food. It has a stiff body and a prehensile tail that it uses when clambering about in bushes and shrubs, although it is equally at home on the ground.

It has a wide range throughout the conifer forests of California and Baja California, and is most common at the edges of fields, especially where there are rocks. It also lives in semidesert habitats and on mountain slopes, but it prefers moist places with some vegetation and ground cover, such as the bottom of canyons and gulleys. It is active during the day even when it is cool and overcast.

Slow and Steady

This species is not the most agile of lizards, owing to the layer of bony plates, or osteoderms, beneath its scales. Unless it is disturbed, it moves at a leisurely pace, inspecting every new thing with its thick, notched tongue. Its gait is deliberate and almost snakelike—pushing itself along with its limbs but also using its body to provide some thrust. It seems to slide gracefully through the vegetation. It is more easily captured than many small lizards, but it is capable of giving a painful bite. It will also part company with its tail at the slightest excuse, sometimes releasing it before it is actually grasped by an enemy.

The southern alligator lizard is an active hunter, foraging for prey among shrubs, leaf litter, and long grass. Its head is wide, and its jaws are powerful, enabling it to crush hard-shelled insects such as beetles. It will also take small vertebrates such as mammals, birds, and

other lizards. Skinks and abandoned skink tails have been found in the stomachs of several specimens.

Reproduction

The lizards breed in the spring. Females may lay two or three clutches of eggs in the course of the summer. However, the northern alligator lizard, *E. coerulea*, which comes from a cooler region but is otherwise similar, gives birth to live young. Both methods have advantages and disadvantages according to circumstances.

There are usually good reasons why some members of a family lay eggs and others give birth to live young. Egg-laying females,

for example, only have to carry their brood for a limited time before laying them. In the case of the southern alligator lizard this means that females can go on to produce one or even two more clutches in the course of a year. Live-bearers have to carry the developing embryos around with them for longer, which may put a strain on them; but they can raise their body temperature by basking, which allows the embryos to develop more quickly. They can also protect them from predators.

Close Relatives

There are eight species in the genus *Elgaria*. Apart from the northern and southern alligator lizards, *E. coerulea* and *E. multicarinata*, another four occur in Baja California (*E. velazquezi*, *E. paucicarinata*, *E. cedrosensis*, and *E. nana*). The latter two are restricted to the small islands of Cedros and Coronado. None have common names, although they are collectively known as *ajolote* in Mexico. The remaining species, the Madrean alligator lizard, *E. kingii*, and the Panamint alligator lizard, *E. panamintina*, live around the Arizona-New Mexico-Mexico borders and in eastern California respectively. Two other alligator lizards are included in the genus *Gerrhonotus*. They are the Texas alligator lizard, *G. liocephalus*, and Lugo's alligator lizard, *G. lugoi* from Mexico.

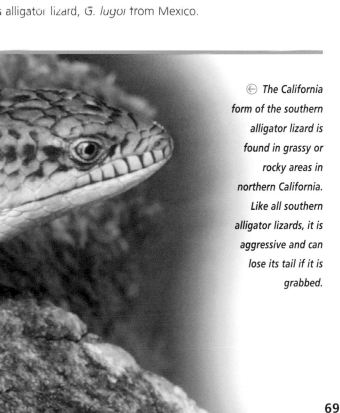

⊖ *The California form of the southern alligator lizard is found in grassy or rocky areas in northern California. Like all southern alligator lizards, it is aggressive and can lose its tail if it is grabbed.*

Xenosaurs

The family Xenosauridae is made up of two genera. One of the most interesting facts about the family is its disconnected distribution—*Xenosaurus* is found in Mexico and Guatemala, while *Shinisaurus* occurs only in southwest China. Although genera within a family often have a wide distribution range, such disjointed distribution is unusual.

In 1928 specimens of a lizard found in China were sent to Germany. Two years later they were described as a new genus and species, *Shinisaurus crocodilurus*, meaning crocodilelike lizard. In 1932 the species was placed in its own family, Shinisauridae. For the next 25 years China was in a period of internal turmoil and isolation, so little interest was shown in the creature. However, studies made by Chinese scientists in the 1960s placed the family Shinisauridae into Xenosauridae, creating two genera with totally separate ranges in the same family. Using the continental drift theory, scientists argued that in the past the continents formed a continuous land mass, and both animals and humans ranged widely. Over millions of years the continents drifted apart, and species became separated. The discovery of *Xenosaurus* fossils in Europe has given credibility to the theory.

The Greek word *Xenosaurus* means "strange lizards" and refers to the problems scientists have encountered in determining their relationships with other lizards and how to classify them. Initially they were thought to be related to the beaded lizards in the family Helodermatidae. Then the presence of osteoderms (bony plates beneath the skin) and lateral folds suggested a link with the family Anguidae; but other differences became apparent, and so they were eventually placed in a family of their own.

Habitat and Behavior

Members of the genus *Xenosaurus* are commonly referred to as knob-scaled lizards. There are five species: *X. arboreus*, *X. grandis*, *X. newmanorum*, *X. platyceps*, and *X. rackhami*.

These secretive lizards have not been the subject of intensive studies, so little is known about their life. Their habitat is the mountain ranges of Mexico and Guatemala, and includes both dry scrub and cloud forest. *Xenosaurus grandis* from southern Mexico is found at higher altitudes than the other species. Although it can be found in arid areas, it spends most of its time in the nearby forests and well-planted sections where humidity and rainfall levels are higher. *Xenosaurus rackhami,* a small xenosaur from the Chiapas region of Mexico, spends most of the day beneath roots in hollow tree stumps, under stones in shallow streams, and in rocky crevices in outcrops in the rain forest. The other species are primarily terrestrial but will sometimes climb about 6 feet (1.8 m) into vegetation. Because they spend some time bathing, they choose spots close to water.

Physical Characteristics

Xenosaurs vary in length from 8 to 16 inches (20–41 cm). *Xenosaurus rackhami* is the smallest, and *X. grandis* is the largest. Their large, deep, flattened head is roughly triangular in shape with strong temporal arches. The strong jaws contain numerous teeth. The eyelids are not

---

Common name Xenosaurs **Family** Xenosauridae

Family Xenosauridae 2 genera and 6 species

Genus *Xenosaurus*—5 species of knob-scaled lizards from Mexico to Guatemala, *X. arboreus*, *X. grandis*, *X. newmanorum*, *X. platyceps*, and *X. rackhami*

Genus *Shinisaurus*—1 species from southwest China, the Chinese crocodile lizard, *Shinisaurus crocodilurus*

 SEE ALSO Alligator and Glass Lizards **46:**50; Lizard, Chinese Crocodile **46:**72; Beaded Lizards **46:**74

movable, and the ear openings (tympana) are covered by scales. The eyes of most species are dark, but *X. rackhami* has bright orange-red irises, which led to the belief among Mexicans that it was related to helodermatids (beaded lizards) and therefore venomous.

The limbs are well developed, and the thin tail is roughly equal in length to the length of the body. The tongue is short, broad, and nicked or slightly forked at the tip. The body is covered with small, granular scales interspersed with larger scales arranged in chevrons across the body. Keeled tubercles in the back and the tail crests contain osteoderms (bony plates). Xenosaurs have cryptic (disguise) coloration with a brown background and lighter "v"-shaped bands in which the tapered tip points toward the rear. The bands are more distinct across the tail. Its forelimbs are yellowish.

Diet and Defense

The lizards are active at dusk and at night. They have a somewhat restricted diet of ants and winged termites, although *X. grandis* also eats some flowers and fruits, and has been seen to take the occasional vertebrate.

Observers report that xenosaurs do not seem to fear humans or other predators. They remain motionless at first and rely on their coloration for camouflage. If this

⊕ *A baby Chinese crocodile lizard,* Shinisaurus crocodilurus, *opens its mouth in a defensive posture.*

fails, they open their mouth to display a black mucous membrane that they use as a warning signal. If the predator does not retreat, they will deliver a bite using their powerful jaws.

Reproduction

For most of the year xenosaurs are solitary creatures. If they encounter other members of their species, fighting breaks out during which a great deal of biting takes place. These lizards breed every other year. Studies of *X. newmanorum* have shown that the number of reproducing females varies from year to year, with 32.5 percent being the lowest recorded and 75 percent the highest. The gender ratio of the lizards has a female bias. However, during the dry season males are more conspicuous than females. Mating takes place in June and July, and females produce live young after a gestation period of 10 to 12 months. Females of *X. newmanorum* have been seen sharing retreats, the young being placed in a "crèche" and guarded by the females until they are several months old.

Common name Chinese crocodile lizard

Scientific name *Shinisaurus crocodilurus*

Family Xenosauridae

Suborder Sauria

Order Squamata

Size 16 in (41 cm)

Key features Top of head flat; raised crest present above the eye and down the back; scales all of the same size and supported by bony plates beneath the skin; legs short and sturdy; claws strong; back and tail brown with yellow to orange underside; males larger than females and more brightly colored with orange sides and throat

Habits Diurnal; spends much of the day motionless in a pool or on a branch in the shade and overhanging water

Breeding Live-bearer; female produces up to 12 live young after a gestation period of 10–14 months

Diet Beetles, insects, fish, crustaceans, slugs, small frogs, tadpoles, and dragonfly larvae

Habitat Cloud forest with dense vegetation and small pools or slow-running rivulets

Distribution Kueilin and Kwangsi Province, China

Status Vulnerable (IUCN); Listed in CITES Appendix II; also protected locally

Similar species None

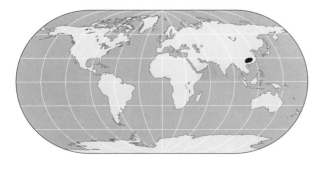

Chinese Crocodile Lizard

Shinisaurus crocodilurus

The Chinese crocodile lizard comes from a small area in the mountains of southwest China, where deforestation is resulting in serious habitat loss for this unusual reptile.

THE CHINESE CROCODILE LIZARD has been known for only about 80 years. The name *Shinisaurus crocodilurus*, meaning "Shin's lizard with a crocodile's tail," was first given to the species in 1930 by a German herpetologist called Ernst Ahl. Shin was the Chinese professor who had collected the first specimens two years earlier. In 1932 the Romanian paleontologist Baron Franz Nopcsa thought the lizard should be placed in a family with the Borneo earless monitor, *Lanthanotus borneensis*. This was based on the fact that they shared common features such as a lack of noticeable ear openings, short limbs, and a crocodile's tail, and had similar aquatic habits. Even recently there has been conjecture as to whether *Shinisaurus* should remain in the family Xenosauridae or be returned to its own family, the Shinisauridae.

Mountainous Habitat

It comes from an area in southwest China south of Guangxi in Kwangsi Province. The main features of the region are the heavily eroded karst mountains, known as the "Mogots," made of limestone formations that rise from the western edge of the south China plain some 650 to 2,500 feet (198–762 m) above sea level. Numerous slow-moving rivulets carve deeply into the rock, which is covered by dense vegetation. It is an area of high rainfall— 80 inches (203 cm) per year. Combined with a maximum summer temperature of 102°F (39°C), the "Mogots" experience humidity of 80 to 90 percent and are shrouded in an almost constant mist. The dense vegetation provides shade and resting sites for the lizard.

→ *The Chinese crocodile lizard has a reputation for remaining motionless for hours or even days on end. When it does move, it is equally at home on land or in water.*

The Sleeping Lizard

Physical Characteristics

Its head is large and boxlike with ridged scales behind the eyes. From the neck to the tail there are quite small, tubercular body scales interspersed with four rows of enlarged, keeled scales supported by osteoderms (bony plates beneath the skin). Scales on the throat are large and slightly raised, creating a granular appearance. The rows of enlarged, keeled dorsal scales meet and form one row on each side of the tail. They resemble a crest, which gives the lizard its common name of crocodile lizard. Its ventral scales are flat, diamond shaped, and arranged in transverse rows.

The thick, muscular tail is slightly longer than the body. Males are larger than females and more brightly colored with orange flanks and throat. In both sexes the back and tail are brown, the ventral surface being pale yellowish to light orange in color. The mouth and throat vary from cream to pale gray with narrow brown lines radiating from the eye to the lips.

Summer Matings

When daytime temperatures fall below 60°F (15°C), Chinese crocodile lizards hibernate in deep vegetation for three to four months. They emerge in March, but mating usually only takes place in August and is initiated by the males chasing the females. At the same time, they bob their head up and down. A receptive female lowers her head, the male bites the nape of her neck to hold her still, and using his

Chinese crocodile lizards are capable of undergoing a metabolic pause during which they remain motionless for hours at a time. Their respiration rate drops, which conserves energy and means they can adapt to sudden cooling without excessive heat loss. This is important, since temperatures in their habitat can fall rapidly at night. Another benefit of reducing the respiration rate is that it helps them stay underwater for long periods. The ability to remain still, combined with their relatively dark body color, helps them blend in with the background (a state known as crypsis).

This behavior led to the Chinese describing *Shinisaurus crocodilurus* as "the lizard of great sleepiness." They believed that the lizard, dried and ground to powder, could cure insomnia, and it was heavily collected for use in traditional medicine.

own tail, raises hers. This allows them to mate. Unreceptive females can inflict quite serious bites on males that persist in trying to mate.

About 10 to 14 months after mating, the females give birth to between seven and 12 live young. If fewer young are produced, they tend to be larger than if many young are born. Youngsters are dark brown with a light-tan snout and forehead.

Beaded Lizards

The Helodermatidae originally contained four genera, three of which are extinct. The remaining genus has two living species, the Mexican beaded lizard, *Heloderma horridum,* and the Gila monster, *H. suspectum.* A third species, *H. texanum*, is extinct.

Helodermatids are venomous lizards that range through the southwestern United States, northwestern and western Mexico, into Guatemala. They are found at varying altitudes from sea level to 4,100 feet (1,250 m). Their habitat is desert and semiarid regions characterized by flat plains of gravel and sand, rocky foothills, and sparse vegetation such as the creosote bush, saguaro, and prickly pear cacti.

If Looks Could Kill...

One of the earliest accounts of beaded lizards was that of a Spaniard in 1577. He wrote, "the bite of this animal, though harmful is not mortal, for which reason it is more dreaded for its appearance than for its bite, and it never tends to harm anyone unless offended or provoked."

The general helodermatid shape is a cylindrical, stout body, a blunt-nosed head, and thick legs. The Gila monster's tail is relatively short and plump. The Mexican beaded lizard has a longer, narrower tail. The stout body is due to bony plates (osteoderms) embedded in the skin. Osteoderms are also found in the skin of crocodiles and alligators. They give extra protection against attack to key vulnerable areas such as the top of the head, the limbs, the back and sides of the body, and the tail.

The tail is used for fat storage and provides a guide to the nutritional state of the lizard. Any food not immediately used for day-to-day activities is converted into fat and stored in the tail. Fatty tissues in the tail also serve to store water, since cell membranes of these tissues can absorb and release water when necessary. The tail may detach if grabbed by a predator; but unlike in true autotomous lizards, it cannot regenerate. The toes have long, curved claws used for digging burrows and climbing.

Beaded lizards have unique, rounded, relatively large raised scales on the upper surfaces resembling beads. The scales do not overlap. Instead, they abut one another and form rows. The scales on the underside are comparatively soft and rectangular.

Feeding and Senses

Beaded lizards eat eggs, insects, earthworms, carrion, lizards, frogs, small mammals, and nestling birds. Their eyesight is poor, and they hunt almost exclusively by taste and smell. The long, forked tongue is constantly flicked out to test the air and the ground, and to carry scent particles to two pits in the roof of the mouth. The pits form the surface layer of a well-developed Jacobson's organ that is sensitive to chemicals. In this way the lizards pick up the odor from nests of birds and mammals. They follow the scent to locate the nest and eat the eggs, nestlings, and young.

Common name Beaded lizards **Family** Helodermatidae

Family Helodermatidae 1 genus, 2 species
Genus *Heloderma*—2 species from southwestern United States and west Mexico to Guatemala, the Gila monster, *H. suspectum*, and the Mexican beaded lizard, *H. horridum*

Misleading Myths

Beaded lizards have been described as big headed, obese, and ugly. Together with the fact that they are the only two venomous lizards in the world, this description has helped fuel various myths that have grown up around them. It is thought that, like the spitting cobra, they are able to spit venom. This belief is based on the fact that, when cornered, a beaded lizard will hiss and gape, and in doing so spray a little saliva. Many people believe that they cannot eliminate their body waste and that this accounts for their foul-smelling breath and venom.

Other myths maintain that their tongue is poisonous, that a beaded lizard will leap on its victims, or that it is a cross between a crocodile and a lizard and that it is impossible to kill because it possesses magical powers. Beaded lizards do have a strong grip, which has given rise to a myth that, once bitten, a victim will not be released until the sun sets or it thunders. The only true fact is that they have a venomous bite.

⟵ *A Mexican beaded lizard,* Heloderma horridum, *lapping up the contents of an egg. The shiny, rounded scales give it the appearance of being studded with hundreds of small beads.*

Since most of their prey is immobile and vulnerable, and the lizards have jaws strong enough to crush it, venom is not needed. However, in association with their warning coloration the venom is an effective means of defense.

Poison Glands

Beaded lizards have venom glands in the lower jaw. Their venom is quite closely related to that of the more primitive snakes, although it is not as potent as that of rattlesnakes or even black widow spiders. The reputation these lizards have for aggression has been greatly exaggerated. They need to be provoked before biting. If they cannot move away, their usual method of defense is to gape and hiss.

Reproduction

Mating in beaded lizards takes place in early to late spring depending on species. Eggs are laid about two months later. In the Gila monster eggs from later matings overwinter to hatch the following spring. Despite this, the lizards breed yearly. Hatching often coincides with the nesting season of many birds and small mammals, thus ensuring an adequate supply of food for the young.

Gila Monster

Heloderma suspectum

Common name Gila monster (Aztec lizard)

Scientific name *Heloderma suspectum*

Family   Helodermatidae

Suborder   Sauria

Order   Squamata

Size   From 13 in (33 cm) to 22 in (56 cm)

Key features Head rounded and bears a patch of light-colored scales; nose blunt; neck short; body heavy with short, powerful limbs and long claws; tail short and fat; scales beadlike; eyelids movable; camouflage colors of black, orange, yellow, and pink on the body; has 2 elongated cloacal scales

Habits   Active by day, at dusk, or at night depending on season and temperatures; spends much of the time in burrows or in shaded areas

Breeding Female lays 1 clutch of up to 12 eggs in late summer; eggs hatch 10 months later

Diet   Small mammals, eggs of birds and reptiles, insects

Habitat   Dry grassland, deserts, and foothills of mountains

Distribution Southwestern United States and northwestern Mexico

Status   Vulnerable (IUCN); listed in CITES Appendix II

Similar species *Heloderma horridum*

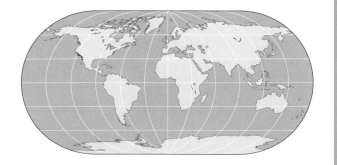

Surrounded by myths and superstitions, the Gila monster is one of just two venomous lizards. Although potent, its venom has hardly ever been known to kill a human.

THE GILA MONSTER is named after the Gila basin in Arizona where numbers of the lizard are plentiful. It is sometimes referred to as the Aztec lizard, since it has featured in paintings by the Aztecs. Although it has a wide distribution in southern Nevada, southeastern California, southwestern New Mexico, and Arizona, numbers are concentrated in small pockets. There are two subspecies: *Heloderma suspectum suspectum*, the Gila monster, and *H. s. cinctum*, the banded Gila monster, which is slightly smaller and whose coloration contains lighter-colored bands. Its range includes southwest Utah and southern Nevada.

The habitat of Gila monsters varies from desert grassland, Mohave and Sonoran desert scrub, to Sonoran thorn scrub. They can be found on lower mountain slopes in arid and semiarid areas and also on adjacent plains and occasionally irrigated areas. They inhabit canyon bottoms—deep ravines with streams that may dry up for part of the year. In parts of Arizona the Gila monster's range extends into oak woodland and in Sonora onto beaches.

Seeking Shade

Within its habitat it seeks shelter under rocks, in dense thickets, and in wood-rat nests. It also digs burrows as well as making use of those belonging to other animals. Although Gila monsters are adapted to an extremely dry habitat, their optimum temperature is only about 86°F (30°C), which is considerably lower than other desert lizards. To avoid the high daytime temperatures during the summer, Gila monsters tend to be active at dawn and dusk. They spend the rest of the day in burrows, often dug using their powerful limbs and long

claws, or under rocks and shrubs. In Arizona Gila monsters spend 98 percent of their active season underground, and in Utah they live for 95 percent of the time in burrows.

During winter when temperatures fall below 50°F (10°C), they hibernate in burrows that have a south-facing entrance. On sunny days they wake and emerge to bask at the entrance. During the rainy season they become active at dusk and nocturnal; but after emerging from hibernation when temperatures are still relatively low, they are diurnal.

The Gila monster has a more rounded head, a shorter tail, and is a smaller species overall than its close relative the Mexican beaded lizard, *H. horridum*. Its long claws are useful when climbing trees, which it frequently does in the rainy season to escape the threat of torrential rain flooding its burrows. In spring it eats insects, but in June and July it changes to small mammals and birds. It can live for several months without food, although loss of weight shows mainly in the tail, which can lose 20 percent of its girth in one month without food.

⊙ *Distinctively patterned in colors of light yellow, orange, pink, and black, the Gila monster is hard to spot against a dark background or in dappled shade.*

Camouflage and Warning Coloration

Coloration of Gila monsters consists of irregular bands and blotches of black, orange, yellow, and pink. Younger specimens have more extensive lighter areas. Unusually for lizards these colors act both as camouflage and as a warning to enemies. Since the Gila monster is active primarily at dawn and dusk, the bands of color are difficult to see in the dappled shade when it moves or shelters beneath creosote bushes and other shrubs. Against a dark background the black markings blend in, and the light markings resemble gravel. Its nose is black, providing excellent camouflage when peering from burrows.

When it moves away from vegetation, its bright body markings become warning coloration, advertising its toxicity. In response to a threat the Gila monster will hiss and gape, revealing the pink venom glands that contrast with the dark lining of the mouth—yet another warning signal.

Beaded Lizard Venom

Venom in reptiles is usually associated with snakes. However, the two species of beaded lizard (the Gila monster and the Mexican beaded lizard) are the only venomous lizards. At first scientists debated whether or not they were venomous and gave the Gila monster the name *Heloderma suspectum*, since at the time it was only suspected to be venomous.

Beaded lizards have 10 teeth in each jaw. When compared with snakes, their venom-delivery mechanism is rather primitive. There is a gland on each side of the jaw with ducts next to the points where the teeth emerge from the jaw. When the animal bites, venom is expelled from the glands some distance from the teeth. The venom flows along a mucous fold between the lip and the lower jaw before reaching the front surface of the teeth. This is an inefficient method compared with the stabbing or biting stroke of vipers and cobras. Instead, Gila monsters must grip the prey or enemy tightly with both jaws and hang on to allow time for the venom to flow into the wound. Its jaws are very strong and difficult to disengage.

The poison produced is a neurotoxin that causes swelling, dizziness, drowsiness, vomiting, palpitations, swollen tongue, paralysis, labored breathing, and a fall in blood pressure. Some people unfortunate enough to have been bitten may experience just one or two symptoms. The swelling and pain that accompany a bite are due to the way in which the venom is injected. The lizard uses its vicelike grip to hold on, and chews with a sideways action of the teeth. It is possible for the elongated, inwardly curved, sharp teeth to break off and remain embedded in the victim. Teeth lost in this way are difficult to detect even using X-rays. Tissue destruction at the site of bites indicates that the venom also contains certain enzymes that play a role in digestion.

Gila venom is classified as sublethal, since there have been relatively few human deaths from it. Exhaustive studies have concluded that only eight to 10 people have ever died from beaded lizard bites. (It is interesting to note that all of them had consumed varying quantities of alcohol.) In the mid 1990s, as a result of studies on beaded lizard venom, pharmaceutical companies began experimenting with new treatments for diabetics based on elements of the venom. Even more recently the venom was found to have memory-enhancing properties, but more research will need to be done on this. Had the Gila monsters not been given protection, such medical advances would not have been possible.

A flaccid tail is an indication of poor condition in a Gila monster. As with other desert creatures, most of the moisture it needs is obtained from its food.

Reproduction

In the mating season Gila monsters have a structured social system in which dominance is established by male-to-male combat. Having spent much of the cooler months hibernating in burrows, they feed voraciously to regain body weight as soon as they emerge. Males become highly territorial in April, and wrestling matches take place. They frequently bite each other but are immune to the venom. Mating occurs in late spring and early summer. In late summer

females lay three to 12 elongated, leathery eggs, which they bury in a sunny spot near a stream at a depth of about 5 to 6 inches (13–15 cm). The eggs overwinter and hatch out about 10 months later.

Endangered Gila Monsters

Gila monsters live in small groups each with a home range of several acres. Although slow moving, they can travel several hundred yards a day. Much of their habitat has been reduced by human encroachment or destroyed by agriculture and industry. Deliberate killing through fear, superstition, or ignorance has depleted numbers further. Many Gila monsters have been collected for the reptile trade, and

some have gone to institutions and serious herpetologists for captive breeding programs.

These lizards have enlarged lungs, which means that they need extra biotin (part of the vitamin B complex) to turn oxygen into carbon dioxide. In the wild this presents no problems, since fertilized eggs containing biotin form part of their diet; but in captivity many have been fed solely on unfertilized hens' eggs that lack biotin, with disastrous results.

Gila monster enjoy a degree of protection. In Arizona it is forbidden to keep them, but the law is not always enforced. They are listed in CITES Appendix II, and pressure is being applied to upgrade the listing to CITES Appendix I to restrict the trade in them still further.

⊕ *Gila monsters grip their prey very tightly in their jaws. Since most of their prey is small and defenseless, venom is not usually needed. Here a Gila monster feeds on a young rodent.*

Common name Mexican beaded lizard

Scientific name *Heloderma horridum*

Family	Helodermatidae
Suborder	Sauria
Order	Squamata
Size	Up to 35 in (89 cm)
Key features	Head rounded; nose blunt; neck quite long; body heavily built; limbs short with long claws on ends of digits; tail long; scales beadlike; eyelids movable; color variable according to subspecies, usually some shade of brown with yellow or cream markings; adults of one subspecies totally black
Habits	Diurnal and nocturnal depending on the weather; also climbs trees; during hot weather spends much of daytime in rocky crevices and self-dug or preexisting burrows
Breeding	Female lays 1 clutch of 7–10 eggs that hatch after 6 months
Diet	Eggs of reptiles and birds, nestlings, small mammals, occasionally lizards
Habitat	Edges of desert, thorn scrub, deciduous woodland
Distribution	Western Mexico and Guatemala
Status	Vulnerable (IUCN); listed in CITES Appendix II; also protected locally
Similar species	*Heloderma suspectum*

Mexican Beaded Lizard

Heloderma horridum

The Latin name for the Mexican beaded lizard means literally "horrible studded lizard." Its body is studded with beadlike scales, each containing a tiny piece of bone that gives it armor-plated skin.

ALTHOUGH THE MEXICAN BEADED LIZARD belongs to the same genus as the Gila monster, *Heloderma suspectum*, there are some differences between the two species. The Mexican beaded lizard is about 13 inches (33 cm) longer and lacks the two elongated cloacal scales. Coloration is also more subdued in the Mexican beaded lizard, and the patch of light-colored scales on the head is absent. Also its tail is longer and more tapering than that of the Gila monster.

The Mexican beaded lizard is more likely than the Gila monster to climb trees to hunt for birds and raid nests for eggs and nestlings. Its tail, which is not prehensile, is used as a counterbalance during hunting. If the tail is lost to a predator, it will not regenerate.

Strong Jaws

The main enemies of the Mexican beaded lizard are coyotes, a few raptorial birds, and humans. Its jaws are strong enough to crush prey, most of which is slow moving, so it is thought that its

⊕ *The Mexican beaded lizard is typically found in dry, open forest areas with plenty of rocks and sparse vegetation. It burrows to avoid the midday heat.*

Names and Legends

It is often thought that the Mexican beaded lizard's scientific name, *Heloderma horridum*, was given partly based on its appearance and partly as a result of its reputation for being venomous. It has been called "one of the most repulsive lizards known to man" and "the terrible one with the studded skin." In Spanish the Mexican beaded lizard is known as El Escorpion. The name comes from a Mexican legend that tells of a beautiful but dangerous creature capable of inflicting its sting on the leg of a human.

venom is used primarily for defense. As with the Gila monster, it gives the impression of being slow moving but is capable of "turning and snapping with the agility of an angry dog" (Ditmars—American naturalist and author).

Humans are responsible for the destruction and fragmentation of considerable tracts of habitat for slash-and-burn agriculture. In the process many Mexican beaded lizards are suffocated in their burrows. Despite protection by CITES and the Mexican government, the creatures still suffer from overcollection for a lucrative, illegal trade. Their venom is no defense against these enemies.

Reproduction

In some parts of its range the Mexican beaded lizard may undergo a short hibernation period; in other parts it remains fairly active during the winter. Mating takes place in early spring. Two months later seven to 10 elongated eggs are laid in a burrow about 5 inches (13 cm) deep. Unlike those of the Gila monster, the embryos are more developed at the time of laying and so do not overwinter. About 6 months later the hatchlings emerge

Identifying the Subspecies

Taxonomists claim that there are four subspecies of the Mexican beaded lizard, although not all are recognized as valid, since the characteristics used to identify them overlap considerably. In 2000, in an attempt to solve the dilemma, a program of genetic analysis using DNA of both captive and wild Mexican beaded lizards was started. The four subspecies have been identified as:

Heloderma horridum horridum—has a wide range in Mexico from Sonora through Oaxaca; coloration is lightish brown with pale yellow or cream markings; the head is darker brown to black

Heloderma horridum exasperatum—ranging widely through southern Sonora and northern Sinaloa in subhumid tropics as well as arid areas; specimens of this subspecies have more yellow than *H. h. horridum*

Heloderma horridum alvarezi—has a restricted range in northern Chiapas and was named after a Mexican botanist; it is smaller than the other subspecies, and although young specimens have the familiar yellow markings, adults lose them and acquire a totally black coloration

Heloderma horridum charlesbogerti—inhabits a relatively small area in the Rio Montagua drainage system; it has larger yellow markings that end at the armpits

Monitor Lizards

Monitor lizards in the families Varanidae and Lanthanotidae are quite closely related to the beaded lizards (Helodermatidae) and the alligator and glass lizards (Anguidae). They are also more closely related to snakes than any other lizard. They are all Old World lizards with a wide distribution in Africa, southern and Southeast Asia, Australia, and islands in the Pacific and Indian Oceans. Most of the species are concentrated in Indonesia and Australia, and in the latter they are referred to as goannas. The Komodo dragon, *Varanus komodoensis*, is the largest living monitor lizard, measuring 10.5 feet (3.2 m) and weighing over 330 pounds (150 kg). The short-tailed monitor, *V. brevicauda,* is the smallest with a total length of 10 inches (25 cm) and weighing just 0.3 ounces (10 g).

Within a relatively few years the number of species of monitor lizards has risen from 40 to 58. This is due to the discovery of new species and the elevation of subspecies to full species. On a number of Asian islands the water monitor, *V. salvator,* and the mangrove monitor, *V. indicus*, have developed a number of forms, all of which seem to be isolated from each other by either a physical or an ecological barrier, creating more confusion.

Varanids arose over 65 million years ago in Asia and spread to Africa and Australia. On the continent of Australia they divided into two forms: One evolved

dwarfism, while the other remained large. The pygmy monitors (the dwarf form) make up the subgenus *Odatria*, while the largest belong to the genus *Varanus*.

Habitats

Monitors have adapted to a variety of habitats ranging from deserts to rain forest, mangrove swamps, and savanna. Their habitat can be divided into four types: aquatic, rocky outcrop, arboreal, and terrestrial.

Some species, such as the sand monitor, *V. gouldii* from Australia, have large ranges and tolerate a variety of habitats. Others exhibit special adaptations to a particular habitat. Merten's water monitor, *V. mertensi* from northern Australia, has a laterally compressed tail to help propel it through water and dorsally positioned nostrils with valves that enable it to lie in the water without choking. A number of species occurring in rocky outcrop habitats have adaptations to their tail scales. King's rock monitor, *V. kingorum* (also from northern Australia), has scales on its lower surface with small, spiny tips that support the lizard's body when at rest in a vertical position. The green tree monitor, *V. prasinus* from Australia and New Guinea, has adaptations for life in the rain-forest canopy. It has a prehensile tail, long claws, and a slender body that is mainly green.

The white-throated monitor, *V. albigularis* from sub-Saharan Africa, is a terrestrial species with powerful limbs for digging. The short-tailed monitor, *V. brevicauda*, spends most of its time in spinifex grass

→ **Monitor lizards are voracious predators, able to tackle even dangerous prey. This savanna monitor,** Varanus exanthematicus **in Kenya, is attacking a spitting cobra,** Naja **species.**

Common name Monitor lizards **Order** Squamata

Family Varanidae 1 genus and 57 species

Genus *Varanus*—57 species in total: 27 from Australia, including the ridge-tailed monitor, *V. acanthurus*, the sand monitor, *V. gouldii*; 4 from Africa, including the Nile monitor, *V. niloticus*; 1 from Arabia; 25 from Asia, Southeast Asia, and Indonesia, including the Bengal or Indian monitor, *V. bengalensis*, and the Komodo dragon, *V. komodoensis*

Family Lanthanotidae 1 genus and 1 species—the Borneo earless monitor, *Lanthanotus borneensis*

SEE ALSO Alligator and Glass Lizards **46**:50; Beaded Lizards **46**:74; Komodo Dragon **46**:94

The Rise and Fall of the Varanids

True monitorlike lizards belonging to the genus *Paleosaniwa* lived more than 65 million years ago and are known from fossils found in Wyoming. About 15 million years later monitors of the genus *Saniwa* developed in the southern United States and northern Europe. While the European species thrived and spread, those in the United States died out. About 5 million years ago the first *Varanus* monitor appeared in India, at the same time as some species in Europe disappeared. Fossil remains in Africa of the semiarboreal *Varanus rusingensis* measuring 6.5 feet (2 m) long show considerable similarities to present-day African monitors such as the Nile monitor, *V. niloticus*.

Monitors reached the continent of Australia comparatively recently (2 million years ago). With a size of 23 feet (7 m) and weighing 1,320 pounds (600 kg) *Megalania*, which inhabited Queensland, New South Wales, and southern Australia, was one of the largest land-dwelling lizards that ever lived. It died out some 25,000 years ago after Australia was occupied by humans. The only remaining genus today in the family Varanidae is *Varanus*.

tussocks using its muscular tail for support. However, it is worth noting that these habitat specializations are not strictly adhered to. Water monitors, *V. salvator*, and Nile monitors, *V. niloticus*, climb trees, dig burrows, and swim.

Most monitors prefer a body temperature of 95 to 104°F (35–40°C). Species such as the white-throated monitor, *V. albigularis*, and the desert monitor, *V. griseus*, which both live in more temperate areas of Africa, are dormant during the winter.

Body Form

Although there is considerable variation in size, the basic body plan of monitors is consistent. Some species have shorter heads and snouts or enlarged scales on the neck, but there is not the dramatic variation in body form and scalation seen in other lizard families.

Monitors have a long neck and body with well-developed limbs, each of which has five toes and long, sharp claws that are curved and bend downward. The tail is long and muscular and can be laterally compressed or rounded and used to store fat. It has no fracture planes, so monitors cannot regenerate a missing part. The head is long with a pointed snout, fairly large ear openings, and eyes with large, round pupils. The teeth are sharp, and the tips point slightly backward. In some species

they are serrated. Body scales are usually small and dull. Species from hotter climates are lighter in color, and juveniles tend to be more colorful than adults.

Behavior, Senses, and Feeding

Monitors occupy large home ranges. When hunting or foraging, they have a swaying gait. They move their head from side to side and tongue-flick constantly. Like snakes, they use their long, protrusible, forked tongue to pick up chemicals in the air to detect food as well as mates.

Monitors are carnivorous predators. They tear flesh with their teeth and claws, and swallow large pieces. The ability to eat large lumps is due to three factors. First, the cranium is completely ossified (protecting the brain from the pressure of a large food item against the roof of the mouth). Second, the large head enables them to make a wide gape; and third, the hyoid bones in the throat are mobile, allowing the neck to be distended considerably. As monitors grow, they eat larger prey. Depending on species and habitat, large monitors eat small mammals, lizards, eggs, birds, fish, crabs, and snakes. Pygmy monitors feed mainly on insects and small lizards.

Most monitors have a clumsy walk. However, they can run fast over distance when chasing prey, since they have large lungs and muscles that store oxygen efficiently. They are opportunistic feeders, and some of them are the top predators, taking the place of large carnivorous mammals. In Australia there are no large predatory cats, and the Perentie monitor, *V. giganteus*, is at the top of the food chain. As its name suggests, it is a "giant," measuring 7 feet (2.1 m) long.

Defense

Habitat destruction by humans is the greatest threat to monitor lizards. They have no defense against it except to try to adapt to different conditions. In this

⊛ The crocodile tree monitor, Varanus salvadorii from New Guinea, uses its narrow snout to look for eggs and fledglings in birds' nests. This is a captive specimen.

Exotic Diets

The pygmy stripe-tailed monitor, *Varanus caudolineatus* from Australia, often tries to capture geckos, although they are too large for it to eat. However, partly as a result of panic and partly to distract the monitor, the geckos "throw away" their tails, leaving behind a tasty meal for the monitor.

White-throated monitors, *V. albigularis* from Africa, are proficient snake hunters and are thought to be immune to the venom in many African snakes. Gray's monitor, *V. olivaceus* from the Philippines, is unusual in that it is a fruit-eating species, although a considerable part of its diet is made up of snails.

The snout of the 10.6-foot (3.2-m) long crocodile tree monitor, *V. salvadorii* from Southeast Asia, is narrow and high, enabling it to forage under bark for vertebrates and to pick eggs and fledglings from nests. Despite its size, it is unable to eat larger prey items.

Dumeril's monitor, *V. dumerilii* from Southeast Asia, eats crustaceans and other hard-shelled items. As a result, its teeth tend to become blunt as the lizard ages.

⊕ *The white-throated monitor,* Varanus albigularis *from Namibia, opens its mouth to pant in an effort to cool down its body temperature.*

respect species that are both arboreal and terrestrial and whose range includes a diversity of habitats are more successful. Young monitors are preyed on by snakes, larger monitors, and raptors.

Monitors have a range of defensive measures. Even the tiny short-tailed monitor, *V. brevicauda*, shows the defensive behavior characteristic of monitors—hissing and swaying with its throat inflated and compressing its body to make itself appear larger.

The tail plays a large part in defense and is often used as a club. Other tactics to deter predators include the violent evacuation of cloacal contents and projectile vomiting, both in the direction of the perceived threat. However, monitors have no defense against the spread of the cane toad, *Bufo marinus*, which is a particular threat in northern Australia. With the exception of the crocodile tree monitor, *V. salvadorii*

from Southeast Asia, all monitors die after eating these toxic toads, resulting in the decline in numbers of some monitor populations.

Reproduction

Male monitors are highly territorial and do not hesitate to fight rivals. Standing on their hind legs, they grab each other with their forelegs, trying to push their rival to the ground. External sexual differences are difficult to detect. Sexual maturity is usually determined by size rather than age, and the female's readiness to breed is directly related to her body length.

All monitors are oviparous, laying eggs in burrows, tree hollows, and even termite mounds. Females of several species dig and open up termite mounds before laying their eggs in them. The insects repair and reseal the gap. Depending on species, about seven to 51 eggs are laid. Eggs of the dwarf monitors hatch after about 65 to 95 days, while the eggs of larger species can take up to 280 or 300 days.

Human Exploitation

For centuries indigenous peoples have hunted monitors for food, medicine, and their skins. In some parts of New Guinea skins of the mangrove monitor, *V. indicus*, are used to make drumhead covers for exportation. In lowland areas of New Guinea other groups prefer to use the skin of the crocodile tree monitor, *V. salvadorii*. The lizards are skinned alive, since they believe that the skin from a live specimen provides a better drum pitch when played. They also believe that the crocodile tree monitor is an evil spirit that is said to "climb trees, walk upright, kill men, and breathe fire."

Australian Aboriginals use the oil from the fat around the kidneys of the lace monitor, *V. varius*, as a remedy for several illnesses. The Aboriginals call it goanna oil. Nile monitors, *V. niloticus*, and Asiatic water monitors, *V. salvator*, are killed for their skins, which are exported for use in making bags, purses, belts, and shoes. Monitors are also collected for the pet trade.

Common name Ridge-tailed monitor
(spiny-tailed monitor)

Scientific name *Varanus acanthurus*

Family   Varanidae

Suborder   Sauria

Order   Squamata

Size   30 in (76 cm)

Key features Body stocky with short legs; head long with
pointed snout; tail very spiny and round in
cross-section; color variable from black to
brown to red

Habits   Spends much of the day sitting on rocks,
basking and foraging among rocks for food;
retreats under boulders at night

Breeding   Female lays 2–3 clutches of 2–11 eggs that
hatch after about 86–92 days

Diet   Mainly insects and some small lizards

Habitat   Rocky areas in tropical and subtropical
habitats

Distribution Northern half of Australia (excluding Cape
York Peninsula) and islands off the northern
and western coasts

Status   Common

Similar species The pygmy ridge-tailed monitor,
Varanus storri, the short-tailed monitor,
V. brevicauda, and the northern blunt-spined
monitor, *V. primordius*

Ridge-Tailed Monitor

Varanus acanthurus

Ridge-tailed monitors come in a variety of colors and sizes. They are unusual among varanids in living in colonies beneath the ground. The young hatch out in the burrows and dig their way to the surface.

THE RIDGE-TAILED MONITOR was first described in 1845 as *Odatria occellata,* but it was renamed *Varanus acanthurus* 40 years later. The name *acanthurus* means spiny tail, which is an alternative common name for the species. It is the largest of a group of ridge-tailed monitors that are found in a variety of habitats ranging from arid to subtropical and tropical areas.

Depending on habitat, the monitor's behavior varies from terrestrial to more arboreal. Individuals from drier parts prefer arid, flat terrain near rocky outcrops. These terrestrial ridge-tails use rocky crevices as retreats or dig their own burrows under large boulders or logs or in dense, low vegetation. Although they bask, they also like to thermoregulate (raise and lower their body temperature as necessary) under cover. In areas where there are no rocks to burrow under, ridge-tails are more arboreal in habit, and they spend the nights and the coolest parts of the year in tree hollows.

Three Subspecies

The species shows three distinct geographical forms that have been classified as subspecies. *Varanus acanthurus acanthurus*, the nominate form, is found in the eastern part of the range and is sometimes called the yellow form. *Varanus a. brachyurus* (which means short tail) inhabits the western part near the Simpson Desert. It has a shorter tail, a slightly larger body, and a yellow stripe runs from the snout through the eye. *Varanus a. insulanicus*

⊖ *The ridge-tailed monitor gets its name from the rows of spines on its tail. The ridged, muscular tail makes a formidable weapon and is also used to protect more vulnerable parts of the monitor's body.*

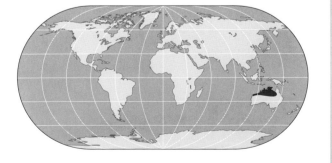

occupies islands off the northern and western coasts, and individuals are darker than the nominate form.

Other differences in structure and color can be seen across the species' wide range. Some of the island specimens are black with yellow ocelli (eye spots); in other parts of the range coloration may be red to brownish orange or yellow with rows of contrasting ocelli, most of which have a black center. Head coloration is usually brown or yellowish brown with paler stripes. Although ridge-tails from some areas have shorter tails than others, red forms have longer tails and a distinct cross-and-spot head pattern.

Communal Living

Ridge-tailed monitors live in underground colonies numbering about 10 to 12 individuals with an alpha (socially dominant) male and female. This is unusual, since most varanids are solitary. The social system of the ridge-tailed monitor includes an alpha female that will attack not only other females but also smaller males.

Ridge-tailed monitors have small, pointed heads. Their body is stocky, and their legs are relatively short. The tail is about one to one and a half times the length from snout to vent. It is ringed with backward-facing, blunt spines. The tail can be used effectively as a whip or club, and the protruding spines can cause a predator to have serious skin abrasions.

With its flat body and spiny tail the ridge-tailed monitor is perfectly evolved for living in burrows and crevices, since it can fill itself with air to avoid being pulled out by a predator. The spiny tail curls around to cover and protect the more vulnerable parts of its body and can also plug the entrance to the burrow. The spines are useful in deterring nocturnal foragers.

The diet of ridge-tailed monitors varies according to season and availability. The main components are beetles, cockroaches, locusts, crickets, and grasshoppers, together with small lizards such as geckos and skinks. Because they have a relatively low metabolic rate, they probably catch most of their food by ambush rather than by pursuit.

Adult ridge-tailed monitors are sexually dimorphic—males have a larger head and thick neck, while females have a more pointed head and slender neck. Adult males also develop clusters of enlarged scales on either side of and just below the vent.

Mating takes place between August and November. Size rather than age determines when females can breed. In the wild females with a head and body length of 4 to 5 inches (10–13 cm) have been found to contain enlarged ova. Gravid females dig an "s"-shaped tunnel beneath a mound, ending with a chamber in which the eggs are laid and incubated. After about three months the eggs hatch during the wet season, and the young dig their way to the surface.

Common name Bengal monitor
(Indian monitor)

Scientific name *Varanus bengalensis*

Family	Varanidae
Suborder	Sauria
Order	Squamata
Size	6 ft (1.8 m)
Key features	Head relatively small and pointed; neck thick and muscular; limbs short; tail long and slightly compressed from side to side; dorsal pattern varies, but basic coloration is black, gray, or brown with lighter markings
Habits	In wet habitats rests on submerged vegetation; in other places climbs trees or forages on the ground; takes refuge in tree hollows, burrows, or termite mounds during inactive periods
Breeding	Mating, egg laying, and hatching vary from region to region; on average female lays 1–3 clutches of a maximum of 30 eggs that hatch after 170–250 days
Diet	Insects, beetles, snails, small amphibians, small mammals, and lizards
Habitat	Variable from rain forest to swamps to more arid, rocky regions as well as cultivated areas
Distribution	Eastern Iran, Afghanistan, Pakistan, India, Nepal, Sri Lanka, Bangladesh, Mayanmar, Malaysia, Sumatra, Java, and the Sunda Islands
Status	Endangered (IUCN) in some parts of its range; listed in CITES Appendix I

Similar species None

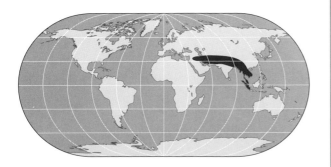

Bengal or Indian Monitor
Varanus bengalensis

For many years the meat and skin of Bengal monitors have been highly prized in areas of India and Asia, a situation that has led to a decline in numbers over parts of their range.

DESPITE ITS COMMON NAME, the Bengal (or Indian) monitor has one of the widest distributions of all monitors. It is found in river valleys in eastern Iran, Afghanistan, and western Pakistan. In the rest of Pakistan it is widespread in various habitats but especially abundant in agricultural areas. It is also found in northern India, Nepal, Sri Lanka, Vietnam, peninsular Malaysia, Java, Sumatra, and the Sunda Islands, where it occurs in habitats as diverse as desert fringes, pristine rain forest, dry open forests, and farmland.

There are two forms of Bengal monitor. *Varanus bengalensis bengalensis*, the nominate form, has larger scales than those of the other subspecies arranged in irregular rows above its eyes. Adults are black, dark gray, or tan to brown with cream or yellowish spots on the back, which vary among individuals. The second form is *V. b. nebulosus*. The scales above its eyes are of differing sizes. Its dorsal pattern is lighter and less distinct, resembling speckling on a light gray to yellowish background. The name *nebulosus,* meaning cloudy, refers to this effect. If there are spots of color, they are tiny, single-scale size. The amount of patterning on an individual seems to be determined by the level of rainfall in its habitat. The plainest individuals are found in desert areas (a feature shared with other monitors in which the lack of any distinct pattern provides better camouflage).

Versatile Lizard

Although mainly terrestrial, Bengal monitors are adept at climbing trees and have been seen dropping to the ground from heights of between 32 and 50 feet (10–15 m) without sustaining any injury. They are also good at running and swimming, and can remain submerged for about an hour. In the more temperate parts of their range activity reduces or halts during the cooler months, although *V. b. nebulosus*, the more tropical form, is active for most of the year. Bengal monitors shelter either in burrows that they dig using their sturdy front legs and claws or in crevices in rocks and buildings. *Varanus bengalensis nebulosus* prefers to seek shelter in tree hollows. Both subspecies also use abandoned termite mounds as hides. Males of the species eat more food than females and are consequently more active. They also grow faster.

The mainly terrestrial Bengal monitor, Varanus bengalensis bengalensis, *will climb into trees in search of food or refuge.*

Compatible Neighbors

Bengal monitors are active in warm habitats. They spend the nights in refuges such as burrows and tree hollows, where their body temperature falls below that of the ambient temperature. Therefore, after emerging from their retreats the following morning, they have to bask for four or more hours to raise their active body temperature to 93°F (34°C). As a result, Bengal monitors tend to be more active and hunt for food in the afternoon, when daytime temperatures are at their highest.

The water monitors, *Varanus salvator*, inhabit the same areas. They spend the night in the water and are able to keep their body temperature higher than the ambient temperature. Since their active body temperature is lower than that of the Bengal monitors—86°F (30°C)—they take less time to warm up and are able to forage for food in the morning. In the afternoon, when the daytime temperature is at its highest, they take refuge in the water to cool off, emerging in the late evening for a final forage. The heat-regulation patterns of these two monitors allow them to coexist in the same area without competing directly with one another.

Water monitors, such as Varanus salvator kabaragoya *from Sri Lanka, live alongside Bengal monitors in many parts of their range. These large monitors can grow up to 8 feet (2.4 m) long.*

Muscular Body

Bengal monitors vary in size according to region and habitat. The total length of specimens in Bangladesh is about 39 inches (100 cm); in Sri Lanka it is 4.6 feet (1.4 m); in Malaysia it is 5.3 feet (1.6 m); and other areas have records of specimens reaching 6 feet (1.8 m) long.

Bengals are characterized by a relatively small, pointed head, a thick, muscular neck, strong limbs, and sharp claws for digging extensive, deep burrows. They can also wedge themselves in the burrows by inflating their body and fixing their claws to the wall. When swimming, they hold their limbs close to their body and propel themselves through the water using undulating body movements and the laterally compressed tail. Their muscular limbs and claws are useful for climbing trees or houses. The tail can be used as a weapon or as a counterbalance when the monitor stands on its hind legs to peer over tall grass.

Foraging for Prey

Although both subspecies feed on the ground, *V. b. nebulosus* will climb trees and is capable of capturing roosting bats. Despite its size and formidable jaws, the creature seems to prefer smaller prey items such as beetles, grubs, grasshoppers, crickets, scorpions, and snails. It licks up ants with its long tongue. Vertebrate prey such as frogs, lizards, small snakes (including cobras), and small mammals appear to be a second choice.

Bengal monitors spend long periods of time rooting in leaf litter for small prey items and have been seen foraging in human garbage. They crush small prey with their powerful jaws, raising their head and throwing the food back into their throat. When eating carrion, they lap up the contents of the digestive tract of herbivorous animals. This is thought to provide additional vitamins and minerals.

Reproduction

Sexual maturity is determined by habitat, food availability, and more importantly, by size. Individuals can take from three to five years to mature (the longer period in less favorable habitats). Females tend to have shorter tails than males; while males have patches of scales arranged as flaps around the anus.

Breeding times vary across the species's range: In northern parts the main reproductive period is during the wet season; in Sri Lanka

Human Enemies

Although young and subadult Bengal monitors may be attacked by other monitor species or by large predatory birds, adult Bengals have few enemies. The greatest danger comes from humans. The monitors are attracted into villages by the presence of poultry and rodents, which make easy pickings. As a result, they are killed by local people protecting their property.

Bengal monitors have been collected on a large scale for their meat and skins. Specimens have been dragged from burrows; their flesh when cooked is supposed to be easy to digest and is used to cure various illnesses. In India, Sri Lanka, Thailand, and Vietnam water monitors, *Varanus salvator*, inhabiting the same range are thought to be inedible, but the Bengal is consumed in large numbers and often forms a major part of the diet of local people. Dark-skinned specimens are particularly sought after. As a result of man's predation, the Bengal monitor can no longer be found in some parts of Sri Lanka, India, and Bangladesh. It is listed in CITES Appendix I, and commercial trade was banned in 1975. However, many countries ignored the ban, and a number of years later Japan was found to be importing hundreds of thousands of skins from Pakistan, Bangladesh, Thailand, and Malaysia.

eggs are laid between January and April; in Thailand, where there is little temperature variation, eggs are produced throughout the year, with some females laying up to three clutches a year. Studies using radio-tracking equipment have revealed that some female Bengal monitors return to the same place each year to lay their eggs.

Depending on the habitat and terrain, eggs may be laid in burrows, termite mounds, tree hollows, or rotten logs. Although the maximum clutch size is 30, *V. b. nebulosus* can average 70 eggs in a year by laying two to three clutches. The incubation period varies between five and nine months.

After hatching, the young monitors tend to hide, often seeking safety in trees and feeding on insects found in the foliage. Juveniles exhibit brighter coloring than their parents, being brownish orange to light brown with bands of black and yellow on the tail and body. It is interesting to note that a clutch of young Bengal monitors remains together as a group for several months before dispersing—there is probably greater safety in numbers.

Sparring Males

Frequent wrestling contests take place as younger males try to secure territories and females. When a rival is spotted, a male rears up on its hind legs, arches its body toward the intruder, lunges, and lashes its tail from side to side. The pair wrestle using their forelimbs.

The scent of a receptive female is present in her feces and is picked up by males in the area. Mating is vicious, the male biting and holding onto the female's neck in order to immobilize her. This means that the most successful males are usually the strongest. In the wild studies have shown that pair bonding plays an important role in the reproduction of Bengal monitors, and there have been many reports of pairs of monitors found together.

⊖ *Looking for all the world as though they were dancing, a pair of Bengal monitors wrestle. The strongest male will win the right to mate with a receptive female.*

Common name Sand monitor (Gould's monitor, "racehorse goanna")

Scientific name *Varanus gouldii*

Family Varanidae

Suborder Sauria

Order Squamata

Size From 4 ft (1.2 m) to 5.3 ft (1.6 m)

Key features Body elongated but stout; head relatively small with pointed snout; tail rounded with dorsal crest on last part; front legs large and strong for digging; coloration variable depending on locality but usually tan to yellow with contrasting spots

Habits Terrestrial with a wide home range; spends much of the day foraging for food; rests in burrows during inactive periods

Breeding Average clutch size of 6–7 eggs laid in excavated nest in soil or in termite mounds; eggs hatch after about 3–4 months

Diet Lizards, small mammals, eggs, and birds

Habitat Subhumid to arid areas, deserts to jungle rivers; generally favors sandy soil; in the north of its range habitat includes tropical woodland

Distribution Most of mainland Australia (except the extreme south and Victoria); recently reported in New Guinea

Status Common

Similar species The Argus monitor, *Varanus panoptes*

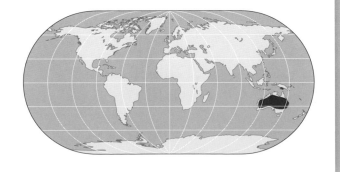

Sand Monitor *Varanus gouldii*

One of the largest Australian monitors, the sand monitor is sometimes known as the "racehorse goanna" because it is capable of extreme speed, often running on two legs over short distances.

DISTRIBUTED OVER MOST of the Australian mainland, the sand monitor is the most widespread goanna. Its habitats vary from the hottest desert areas to humid tropical forest. Sand monitors like to dig at the base of low vegetation, using their long, stout claws to excavate a sloping burrow with an expanded chamber at the end.

Although they swim reasonably well, they are unable to remain under water for more than a few minutes. They are mainly terrestrial and not very good at climbing. But if that is the only means of escape, they overcome their reluctance. Activity levels are seasonal. During the warm months (September to February) they are very active. From March to August activity levels fall dramatically, and they spend most of the time in burrows or tree hollows.

Sand monitors are capable of standing and running on their hind legs. This is known as bipedalism and appears to have evolved in a few monitor species partly to allow the creatures to look over tall vegetation or rocks. In the case of males they use this stance to grapple with rivals. While bipedal locomotion is fast, it cannot be sustained for very long.

Taxonomy

Two subspecies are recognized: *V. gouldii flavirufus*, which inhabits true sandy deserts and is the smaller of the two, and *V. gouldii gouldii*, which is found in areas with more rainfall and more vegetation. The latter is larger, since its habitats have higher densities of prey.

Sand monitors have a long, stout body with a small head and a pointed snout. The long, muscular front legs end with sharp claws and are ideal for digging in hard ground and into mammal tunnels. The tail is compressed from

Hunting Methods

side to side and helps in swimming. Color can be dark brown or black to light yellow and reddish. Large pale spots form rows between the neck and the base of the tail. The tail is paler with narrow bands, and the last part has no markings. A dark, white-edged streak runs from the eyes to the ears. These colors provide camouflage in desert areas and among grasses.

Sand monitors are opportunistic feeders, taking whatever they can whenever they can. Although they have been seen to eat carrion, they prefer to capture live prey, such as geckos,

Sand monitors hunt mainly by smell. They forage for over 1.2 miles (2 km) a day. In desert areas where food densities are low, *V. g. flavirufus* needs to travel farther in search of food. The monitors search for scent trails by swinging their long neck and head from side to side in a large arc, covering as much ground as possible, and constantly flicking out their long, forked tongue.

When they pick up a scent, they follow it to its source—usually a burrow. They use their front legs to dig up the prey, making sure they keep their head well down with their sharp teeth at the ready to snatch up the prey before it can escape.

⊖ *Spreading its feet wide and raising itself to its full height, a sand monitor stands on its hind legs to look over tall grass or bushes. As it does so, it constantly flicks its tongue to test the air for scents.*

other lizards, some of the pygmy monitors, as well as young of their own species. They also eat reptile eggs, baby mammals, and young birds. In the northern part of their range they readily consume cane toads, *Bufo marinus*, but they are vulnerable to the toads' toxins and often die as a result.

Because they can grow up to 5.3 feet (1.6 m), adult sand monitors have few enemies. Juveniles are more vulnerable. When cornered, sand monitors inflate their throat, rise up on their hind legs, hiss, and lunge at their aggressor. They are frequently caught by Aboriginals who kill them and cook them.

Little is known about reproduction in the sand monitor. Mating has been observed during October to December. Eggs are laid in burrows dug in hard soil, inside tree stumps, or occasionally in termite mounds. Incubation time is thought to be about three to three and a half months, and the hatchlings emerge in January to March. Juveniles are more brightly colored than the adults.

Common name Komodo dragon

Scientific name *Varanus komodoensis*

Family   Varanidae

Suborder   Sauria

Order   Squamata

Size   Up to a maximum of 10.3 ft (3.1 m)

Key features Body very large; head relatively small; ear
                 openings visible; teeth sharp and serrated; tail
                 powerful; strong limbs and claws for digging;
                 scales small, uniform, and rough; color varies
                 from brown to brownish or grayish red;
                 juveniles are green with yellow-and-black
                 bands

Habits   Spends much of the time foraging for food;
                 digs burrows to which it retreats at night and
                 during hot weather

Breeding   Female lays clutch of up to 30 eggs
                 (depending on size of female); eggs buried in
                 earth and hatch after 7.5–8 months

Diet   Insects, reptiles, eggs, small mammals, deer,
                 goats, wild boar, pigs

Habitat   Lowland areas ranging from arid forest to
                 savanna, including dry riverbeds

Distribution Islands of Komodo, Rinca, Padar, and
                 Western Flores in Indonesia

Status   Vulnerable (IUCN); listed in CITES
                 Appendix I; protected locally

Similar species None

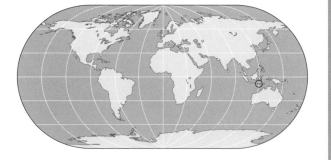

Komodo Dragon

Varanus komodoensis

*Growing to just over 10 feet (3 m) long, the
Komodo dragon is the largest lizard in the
world. Up to 5,000 Komodos are restricted
to a few small islands in Indonesia,
where they reign supreme.*

THE KOMODO DRAGON IS KNOWN LOCALLY as the *ora*
or *buaja daret*, meaning land crocodile, and is
named after a mystical dragon famed for its
size and ferocity. The total area occupied by
these monitors is about 390 square miles
(1,000 sq. km). It is found on the Lesser Sunda
Islands of Rinca, Komodo, and Flores and the
smaller islands of Gili, Montang, and Padar,
although the latter does not have a permanent
population. All the islands except Flores are
now part of the Komodo National Park.

   The native habitat of Komodo dragons
consists of arid, volcanic islands with steep
slopes. At certain times of the year water is
limited, but during the monsoon
season there may be some
flooding of the area. Average
daytime temperatures are 80°F
(27°C). Komodos are abundant in
the lower arid forests, savanna, and thick
monsoon forest near watercourses. Adults
prefer the more open areas of savanna with tall
grasses and bushes. Hatchlings and juveniles are
more arboreal and tend to stay in forested
regions, where they spend much of the time on
branches away from would-be predators.

⊕ *Despite their
enormous size and
weight, Komodo dragons
are quite fast runners
and can swim well.
Young Komodos are also
adept at climbing.*

Largest Lizard

Although the Crocodile tree monitor, *Varanus
salvadorii* from New Guinea may be slightly
longer (due to its long, slender tail) and weighs
up to 200 pounds (90 kg), the Komodo dragon
is classed as the world's largest living lizard. It
weighs up to 330 pounds (150 kg). Its head is
relatively small when compared with its large,

stout body. Unlike in many other monitor species, the nose is somewhat rounded and blunt. External ear openings are visible. The strong jaws, which are capable of crushing bones, contain 60 laterally compressed teeth with serrated edges (similar to those of flesh-eating sharks), which can be replaced many times. The highly flexible skull allows the monitor to swallow large pieces of food, and the muscular, powerful legs end with clawlike talons that are ideal for ripping open carcasses. A heavy, muscular tail makes an additional weapon to help overcome prey and is capable of delivering a crushing blow.

The body of a juvenile Komodo is more sinuous and, together with its sharp claws, enables it to pursue an arboreal lifestyle. Green background coloration with pale yellow-and-black bands provide effective camouflage against the foliage. Juveniles lead secretive lives,

Discovering the Dragons

Although there had been tales of "monsters" on Indonesian islands, it was only early in the 20th century that serious consideration was given to mounting an expedition to search for them. This was after a Dutch pilot had crashed in the area and taken back to the West information from tribes in the Lesser Sunda Islands about "huge monsters—land crocodiles more than 20 feet [6.1 m] in length." An expedition led by Major P. A. Ouwens, director of the Zoological Museum in Buitenzorg, Java, produced the first scientific description of the dragons; shortly after, in 1912, the Indonesian government closed the area. Hunting of the dragons was outlawed, and the numbers sent to zoos were restricted. However, myths of enormous 20-foot (6.1-m) dragons persisted.

After an exhaustive study of the creatures in the wild, in 1981 the American paleontologist Walter Auffenberg recorded the largest specimen encountered as 9.8 feet (3 m) long. To date the largest authenticated Komodo dragon is a 10.3-foot (3.1-m) male. It died in 1933 and is on display at the Tilden Regional Park in Berkeley.

Despite the existence of the dragons, dangerous felons were once exiled on Komodo Island. The survivors built Komodo village, which makes most of its money today from tourism and fishing.

spending most of their time foraging in trees, avoiding predation by adults. As they grow and become too heavy to live in trees, their diet alters, and they become more terrestrial.

Adult Komodos lose the juvenile sinuousness to become robust creatures. The rough scales give the skin a beaded appearance, and coloration changes to brown or reddish gray. Some individuals may have darker limbs and a patch of peach color around the eyes. Both adults and juveniles have a yellow tongue. Despite their size and weight, Komodos can move surprisingly quickly and are excellent swimmers. Some of the populations on the smaller islands are transient, swimming from island to island in search of food.

Top Predator

Much of the Komodo dragon's day is spent patrolling its territory. The core range containing burrows may cover an area of 1.2 square miles

⊕ *A keen sense of smell enables Komodo dragons to seek out carrion from several miles away. Tearing at a carcass with their sharp teeth, the feast is soon over.*

Attacking and Scavenging

The Komodo dragon obtains food both by attacking and by scavenging. Using ambush techniques, it hides in the long grass along well-used mammal trails. To be successful, the monitor needs to be within 3 to 5 feet (1–1.5 m) of its prey. Rushing from its hiding place, it seizes a leg, and its sharp teeth sever the tendons to disable the prey. The dragon then kills its victim by a bite to the throat or by using its sharp claws to rip out its intestines. Should a victim escape after the first bite, it may still die. Initially, Komodo dragons were thought to be venomous. However, it is now known that their saliva (of which they produce copious amounts) contains 57 types of bacteria (seven of which are extremely infective) and an anticoagulant—all acquired as a result of eating carrion.

Eventually the prey succumbs either from shock, blood loss, or infection. The smell of its rotting body can easily be detected by other dragons from as far away as 5 miles (8 km). When several Komodos find carrion, a complex social structure is observed. Using their serrated teeth to rip off large chunks, large males eat their fill first, followed by smaller males and females. Any juveniles in the area wait until the larger dragons leave before descending from the trees to scavenge on any leftovers. A Komodo dragon can eat up to 80 percent of its body weight in one meal. It has been estimated that only 13 percent of a corpse is left by Komodos—the intestines, fur, and horns are the only parts not eaten.

⬆ *Komodo dragons are now the focus of a growing tourist industry. In some areas of Komodo Island the dragons are so well fed that they just lie around waiting for tourists to bring the next meal of goat or sheep. However, their future surivival is threatened by habitat destruction.*

(2 sq. km), but feeding ranges, which may be shared, extend farther. It is not unusual for a dragon to cover 6.3 miles (10 km) in a day. Burrows are used to regulate body temperature. They enable the dragon to cool down during the hottest part of the day and serve as retreats for shelter and warmth at night, since they retain some of the daytime heat.

Komodo monitors are formidable predators at the top of the food chain. Juveniles feed on grasshoppers, beetles, small geckos, eggs, and birds, and move up to small mammals as they grow. Adults consume a variety of large prey, all of which has been introduced to their islands by humans, including goats, pigs, deer, wild boar, horses, and water buffalo. Smaller, weaker dragons make up about 10 percent of an adult's diet. Eye witness accounts tell of an adult Komodo eating a 90-pound (41-kg) pig in 20 minutes; on another occasion one ate a 66-pound (30-kg) boar in 17 minutes!

Courtship and Monogamy

Courtship rituals have been observed in most months of the year, but mating activity peaks in July and August. When they are ready to mate, female Komodos give off a scent in their feces that is detected by a male when patrolling his territory. He follows the scent until he locates the female and then sniffs all over her body. He rubs his chin on her head, scratches her back, and licks her body—

tongue-licking gives him clues to her degree of receptivity. The female communicates that she is ready to mate by licking the male. Grasping her with jaws and claws, he lifts her tail with his, which allows him to mate. An unreceptive female hisses, inflates her neck, bites, and lashes with the tail to drive away the male.

Up to 30 eggs are laid either in a specially dug nest chamber and covered with earth and leaves or in a burrow. Female Komodos have been seen to use the nest mounds of the male brush turkey. By adding or removing material, the male bird keeps the mound in which his mate's eggs are laid at a constant temperature, making an ideal incubator for Komodo eggs. The hatchlings emerge about 8 months later and measure 15 inches (38 cm). Mortality rates are high, with many falling prey to larger Komodos, predatory birds, snakes, and feral dogs. As soon as possible, the hatchlings try to make for the trees and comparative safety.

It is interesting to note that monogamy (having only one mate) and courtship displays have been observed in many Komodo dragons. These large monitors are capable of inflicting fatal wounds and readily eat members of their own species. Therefore it would seem that pair bonding in this way enables them to recognize certain individuals and ensures the continuation of the species.

Dragons in Danger

There are estimated to be between 3,000 and 5,000 Komodo dragons in the wild, and males outnumber females 3 to 1. They have been placed on CITES Appendix I to control trade in them, but occasionally specimens are smuggled out illegally. The Indonesian government has also given them the highest level of protection, and they are regarded as "national treasures." They are classed as Vulnerable by IUCN. The threat to their survival comes from habitat destruction and poaching of their prey: Volcanic activity and natural fires can have a serious effect on their already restricted distribution, and the poaching of their prey by humans may also have serious consequences for the dragons.

Common name
Nile monitor

Scientific name *Varanus niloticus*

Family   Varanidae

Suborder   Sauria

Order   Squamata

Size   Up to 6.5 ft (2 m)

Key features Body elongated with muscular limbs and
sharp claws; skin tough with small, beadlike
scales; tail laterally compressed; basic
coloration olive-green to black with variable
lighter markings

Habits   Spends nonhunting daylight hours basking on
rocks and branches or in water; uses burrows
and old termite mounds at night; can swim
well

Breeding   Female lays up to 60 eggs in a clutch, often
in termite mounds; eggs hatch after 150–200
days

Diet   Insects, eggs, birds, small mammals,
crustaceans, amphibians, snakes, lizards

Habitat   Grassland, fringes of deserts, rain forests,
even cultivated areas—almost anywhere
providing there is a permanent body of water

Distribution Eastern and southern Africa from Egypt to
South Africa

Status   Common

Similar species None

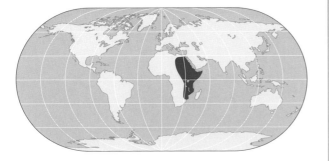

Nile Monitor *Varanus niloticus*

*Nile monitors are most often seen basking on rocks
and branches or in the water. Adults can easily outrun
humans over short distances even over open ground
and will invariably head for water when pursued.*

THE NILE MONITOR IS THE LARGEST LIZARD in Africa and
probably the most widespread. Although absent
from deserts, it is found wherever there are
permanent bodies of water. It is common in all
major river valleys and is often seen foraging for
food in vegetation at the edge. In more
temperate areas Nile monitors bask on rock
outcrops, tree stumps, or branches overhanging
water. They spend periods of the day partly
submerged. In areas where water is present,
Nile monitors remain active all year. Burrows,
abandoned termite mounds, tree hollows, and
caves within rock piles are used as nighttime
retreats and during the dry season or in cooler
months when activity is reduced.

There are two subspecies: *Varanus niloticus
niloticus* (which has six to nine yellow dorsal
bands and a bluish-black tongue) and *Varanus
niloticus ornatus* (which has three to five
yellow bands and a pink tongue). The latter
prefers higher humidity and slightly cooler
temperatures, and is restricted to the rain
forests and coastal grasslands of central and
western Africa. The general background
coloration of both subspecies is olive-green to
black with yellowish chevrons on the skull.

Agile Hunters

Nile monitors are quick, agile creatures with
crushing jaws and powerful, claw-tipped limbs
that make them efficient predators. Although
they feed on carrion and forage in human
garbage dumps, they get most of their food by
hunting. To locate prey, they use vision and the
tongue, the latter carrying scent particles to the
Jacobson's organ in the mouth. Since prey varies
with habitat and the season, Nile monitors tend
to be omnivorous. They feed on insects, snakes,

Nile Monitors and Crocodiles

lizards, fish, small mammals, birds, eggs, mollusks, and amphibians. They forage on and below ground, in trees, and in water.

As they age, changes occur in the structure of their teeth and skull. Young Nile monitors eat mainly active prey such as insects and lizards and have sharp, pointed teeth. Over time they are replaced with broader, blunter teeth. These changes occur as the monitors move to more sedentary prey with armor plating, such as crabs, mollusks, and turtles, which have to be crushed before they can be swallowed.

Some people believe that the Nile monitor is a more dangerous adversary than a crocodile of a similar size. With sharp claws and teeth and a powerful tail that it uses as a club, it can defend itself against most (but not all) predators. Large crocodiles, pythons, and cobras can overpower and kill a monitor. Monitors also come into conflict with humans when they raid poultry stocks, and they are hunted by humans.

Nile monitors are important predators on crocodile nests, eggs, and young. Although a monitor usually digs up an unguarded nest, studies of their behavior in the wild show that monitors will cooperate with each other to raid a nest guarded by a female crocodile. While one monitor draws the crocodile away from the nest, its accomplice digs up the eggs. When an egg is located, the monitor grasps it between its jaws, raises its snout in the air, and cracks the egg, thus ensuring that both contents and shell slide down the throat with no waste. Large specimens eat eggs whole. Young crocodiles hiding at the edges of rivers are easy targets for Nile monitors; by preying on them, the monitors play an important role in controlling crocodile numbers.

⤵ *Nile monitors are omnivores and often forage near water. Their strong teeth are adapted for crushing the shells of any mollusks or bivalves they encounter, such as these oysters in Tanzania.*

Their flesh is eaten, their organs and tissues are used in traditional medicine, and their skins are exported to make various leather-type goods.

Reproductive Behavior

Male Nile monitors are highly territorial and may rear up on their hind legs to engage in combat during the mating season. In other varanids the fight is over when the losing male retreats, but the victorious male Nile monitor inflicts painful bites on its defeated opponent. Mating and egg-laying times vary with location. In Senegal eggs are laid during the wet season in October to December. Gravid females have been found in Ghana in August and September, in Zanzibar in July, and in Tanganyika in November. Incubation periods vary depending on temperature, but on average the young hatch out over several days about 150–200 days after the eggs have been laid. They are sustained at first by the attached yolk sac. It is thought that the young that hatch from eggs laid in termite mounds eat termites for their first meal.

Borneo Earless Monitor

Lanthanotus borneensis

The Borneo earless monitor is in a family of its own. This unique lizard was once thought to be the missing link between snakes and lizards, but the theory has since been rejected.

THE BORNEO EARLESS MONITOR was first described in 1878, but many aspects of its life remain a mystery today. It was originally considered to be a relative of the Gila monster, *Heloderma suspectum* (Helodermatidae). Research in the 1960s suggested that a creature resembling the earless monitor with a subterranean lifestyle, small eyes, absence of ear openings, elongated body, forked tongue, and recurved (backward-pointing) teeth was the ancestor of snakes. However, 10 years later the conclusion was reached that although *Lanthanotus borneensis* has many snakelike features, so do other lizards. It is now known that this creature is not the missing link between snakes and lizards.

Family Likenesses

Which family the Borneo earless monitor should be placed in has been the subject of much debate. The Austrian zoologist Franz Steindachner, who discovered the lizard, thought that it was so different from any other lizard that he placed it in a family of its own, the Lanthanotidae. The validity of this was later questioned by a Belgian, George Boulanger, who felt that it should be possible to assign the creature to an existing family. Based on shape, scalation, tongue, and limb size, he put it in the family of beaded lizards, the Helodermatidae.

It was only many years later that studies of a dead specimen showed that the Borneo earless monitor lacks grooved teeth and venom glands—which are characteristics of the beaded lizards. New methods used to study relationships between groups of lizards and aid classification suggest that *Lanthanotus* is more like the true monitors, and it has been assigned to a family of its own.

Common name Borneo earless monitor

Scientific name *Lanthanotus borneensis*

Family   Lanthanotidae

Suborder   Sauria

Order   Squamata

Size   From 17 in (43 cm) to 20 in (50 cm)

Key features Nose blunt; tail as long as body; eyes small; no external ear openings; rows of dorsal scales are keeled and interspersed with smaller, granular scales

Habits   Active at dusk and at night; spends much of the time either in burrows in riverbanks or in the water; semiaquatic and a burrower

Breeding   Female lays 1 clutch of up to 6 eggs

Diet   Thought to include worms, fish, and eggs

Habitat   Riverbanks in rain forest and also shallow water in rice paddies

Distribution Sarawak and Borneo

Status   Vulnerable (IUCN)

Similar species None

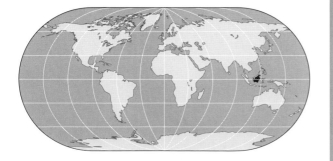

The Borneo earless monitor inhabits rain forest in Sarawak and Borneo, and often frequents ditches in rice paddies. Since it is a burrower and semiaquatic, it is rarely seen by humans except during seasonal floods. During the day it retreats to burrows dug in moist soil near riverbanks.

A good swimmer, it has translucent lower eyelids and valvular nostrils that enable it to remain submerged for up to an hour. It can also slow down its metabolic rate for up to 24 hours, an ability similar to that of the Chinese crocodile lizard, *Shinisaurus crocodilurus*. This trick is useful for a creature living in burrows that may flood. It can reduce its breathing until it can escape or until the floodwater recedes.

Subterranean Adaptations

The earless monitor has other adaptations to life below ground and in the water. Its long, cylindrical body and tail are covered with large, keeled scales that form longitudinal rows from neck to tail. They are interspersed with smaller

⊕ *The body form and granular scales of the Borneo earless monitor are reminiscent of the beaded lizards in the family Helodermatidae. However, it differs in having no external ear openings and nostrils that are positioned almost on top of the head.*

granular scales. The flat head with its small scales, blunt snout, tiny eyelids, lack of ear openings, and nostrils situated almost right on top is an ideal tool for burrowing in moist soil. Its legs are short and thick with five clawed digits each. Although the tail is a little prehensile, the earless monitor has not been seen to climb. Brown coloration provides effective camouflage.

Since it is largely active at dusk and at night, the feeding habits of the earless monitor are poorly known. Its mouth is comparatively small, and it is thought to eat mainly worms and small fish. It may also suck out the contents of eggs belonging to birds that nest close to the water's edge.

Very little is known about reproduction, including mating behavior and incubation time. Studies show that the male has a blunt, more rectangular jaw than the female and a thicker tail base. Mating is thought to take place in the water. Eggs taken from preserved specimens are 1.3 inches (3 cm) long and are laid in a clutch of up to six, although three to four seem to be more common. It would appear that no eggs have been laid and hatched in captivity.

WORM LIZARDS

The worm lizards form a separate suborder in the order Squamata—the Amphisbaenia. The name Amphisbaenia means "to go both ways" and refers to their blunt head and tail, which are easily confused. Their closest relatives are the lizards and snakes, and they are assumed to have come from a common ancestral line, although their origins have not been established. They share certain characteristics with some lizard families (geckos, skinks, and anguids) and others with snakes. They differ from snakes and legless lizards in that their right lung is reduced or absent. (Nearly all other elongated reptiles have reduced left lungs.) They are among the least studied reptiles, and even the basic natural history of most species is completely unknown.

All amphisbaenians are long with short tails. Three species in the genus *Bipes* have front limbs, but the others are all legless. They are characterized by the rings (known as annuli) that are formed by their square-shaped scales. In most species two annuli correspond to each vertebra, except in the genus *Blanus*, which is thought to be a primitive lineage, and whose members have one annulus per vertebra.

All worm lizards have tiny inconspicuous eyes covered with scales, which show up as a pair of small dark spots. They can distinguish light from dark but are unable to produce an image. They have no external ear openings, and their nostrils point backward. Most species are pink or white, but some have patterns of darker pigment. At first glance they look like earthworms, a similarity that is not coincidental. Like earthworms, amphisbaenians are exclusively burrowers.

Tunneling Machines

Their physical features (or rather the lack of them) are all associated with a subterranean existence. They spend their entire lives below ground living in tunnel systems that they construct themselves. They have heavily reinforced, rigid skulls with which they dig tunnels through the soil, which can be quite hard in some cases.

There are three basic skull designs. First, many species, such as the Iberian worm lizard, *Blanus cinereus*, and the South American sooty worm lizard, *Amphisbaenia fuliginosa*, have bullet-shaped or conical heads that they use simply to ram their way through the soil. This is thought to be a primitive feature, and it restricts these particular species to loose, friable (crumbly) soils. Others, such as the African *Monopeltis* species (Amphisbaenidae), have flattened, shovel-shaped heads covered by a bony plate with a hard cutting edge. Having made an impression with their pointed snout, they use the cutting edge to scrape soil away before compacting it against the side of the tunnel by moving their head up and down. Third, there are the keel-headed species, such as the Brazilian *Anops* species and the Tanzanian *Ancylocranium* species, in which the head is compressed from side to side. They compact the soil by swinging their head left and right as they go. Members of one small family, the Trogonophidae, which live in sandy soil, rotate their head first one way and then the other to shave the sides off their tunnels and to compact the walls, so they appear to twist their way through the ground.

Digging tunnels using any of the methods described can be a slow, laborious process; but once a tunnel system has been constructed, the worm lizard can move through it rapidly. A worm lizard moves along its tunnel by sliding its loosely attached skin forward over the body itself (like pulling up the sleeve of a sweater). It then uses the outer surface, perhaps helped by the annuli, to brace itself against the sides of the tunnel. At the same time, it pulls the inside cylinder of its body forward using muscles connecting the body wall to the inside surface of the skin.

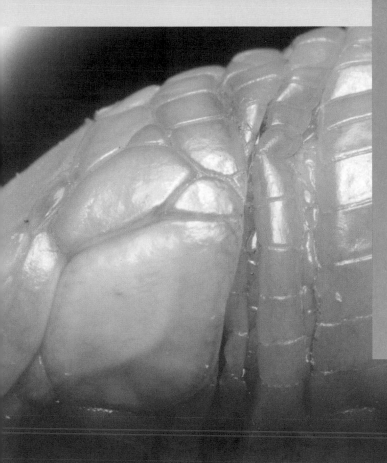

⤢ *This worm lizard from southern Africa shows the shovel-shaped head and the fused eyelids that are typical of many amphisbaenians. Its strong head and snout are used to construct and enlarge burrows.*

When a worm lizard moves purposefully, this two-stage process occurs along the length of its body, so the overall impression is of a rippling effect.

⤢ *Tunneling techniques. The shovel-snouted species (1) and the keel-snouted species (2) use similar methods: At the start of the stroke (1a, 2a) the scale rings behind the head are close together. As the worm lizard rams the end, the rings separate, and the head is pushed forward (1b, 2b). Tunnel widening is achieved by lifting the head against the tunnel roof (1c), or bending the head downward (2c), or around the back of the skull by bending the body sideways (2d).*

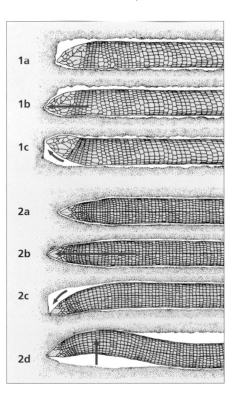

Life Underground

Worm lizards presumably move around inside their tunnel systems to look for food and mates, but they also use the galleries to thermoregulate. Temperature variations occur in parts of the tunnel system according to whether they are in the open or in the shade and how near the surface they are.

In cool weather worm lizards can be found near the surface, often where a tunnel emerges under a flat rock or log; but in hot, dry weather they are impossible to locate without digging because they retreat to lower levels. Worm lizards sometimes emerge onto the surface to feed at night, but they are normally only seen if heavy rains have flooded their burrows and forced them out.

They obtain their food in three different ways. First, invertebrates such as earthworms and insect grubs may fall into their burrows by accident. Second, the tunnel system may extend into an area of soil that includes a nest of insects such as ants or termites. And third, the worm lizards may wait in burrows just beneath the surface to ambush invertebrates and small vertebrates that walk overhead. Some species, such as the ajolote, *Bipes biporus* from Mexico, are highly sensitive to the slightest movement overhead. They break through the surface to grasp their prey and drag it under the ground.

Specialized Enemies

Enemies of worm lizards include snakes such as the coral snakes, *Micrurus*, that track them along their tunnels. Some coral snakes seem to specialize in hunting worm lizards and are probably their main predators in places. In Africa quill-snouted, purple-glossed, and wolf snakes (*Amblyodipsas, Xenocalamus,* and *Lycophidion* species) probably fill a similar niche wherever there are enough worm lizards.

As in some lizard species, small worm lizards with long tails can discard the end of their tail (known as autotomy). The discarded tail then forms a plug in the tunnel, keeping the predator from following the fleeing worm lizard (or providing it with a small meal while the worm lizard escapes). Since they cannot grow a new tail, small worm lizards can use the strategy only once. Large worm lizards have short tails and cannot autotomize.

Reproduction

Most worm lizards lay eggs, but there are exceptions. The checkered worm lizard, *Trogonophis weigmanni* from North Africa, the five *Chirindia* species from East Africa, the Cape shovel-snouted worm lizard, *Monopeltis capensis*, and the Tanzanian *Loveridgea ionidesi* all give birth to live young. Egg-laying species sometimes use ant or termite nests in which to lay their eggs; the temperature and humidity are carefully controlled by the insects, and there is a ready supply of food for the newly hatched young. Much of this is speculation, unfortunately, since almost nothing is known about their life histories.

The Families

There are three families within the suborder, but only one is easily distinguished by superficial characteristics. This is the Bipedidae, which differs from all the others in that its members have two front legs. The others have no legs at all. The distribution of worm lizard families is interesting. The large family Amphisbaenidae is found across the tropical regions of South America and the southern half of Africa but also has outlying species in North Africa, southern Europe, and the eastern Mediterranean. The two smaller families are widely separated from the Amphisbaenidae: The Bipedidae is found in western Mexico and the Trogonophidae in North Africa, the Horn of Africa (Somalia), and the Arabian Peninsula.

The Amphisbaenidae is the largest family. Among its 155 species is the largest of all worm lizards, the white worm lizard, *Amphisbaenia alba* from South America. It is a large stocky white or reddish-brown species that grows to about 30 inches (75 cm) and lives in rain forests, where it eats large invertebrates and small vertebrates. Other members of the genus are found throughout South

⬅ *The distinctively patterned checkered worm lizard,* Trogonophis weigmanni, *lives in the arid sandy environment of Morocco. It is unique in the Trogonophidae for giving birth to live young.*

⬇ *The largest of all amphisbaenians is the white worm lizard,* Amphisbaenia alba *from South America (Amphisbaenidae). It lives in rain forests and grows to 30 inches (75 cm) long.*

America, and there are some on the larger islands in the West Indies.

The other large genera are *Cynisea,* with 17 poorly known species from West Africa, and the shovel-snouted worm lizards, *Monopeltis,* with 19 species from central and southern Africa. The Cape shovel-snouted worm lizard, *M. capensis,* gives birth to one, two, or three live young, but the reproductive methods of the others are unknown. *Blanus* is a small genus of four species from southern Europe, Turkey, and North Africa. The Florida worm lizard, *Rhineura floridana,* is the only member of its genus. It occurs exclusively in Florida and Georgia, and is the only worm lizard in the United States, where it is endemic.

Members of the Trogonophidae are known as short-headed worm lizards. They have a broken distribution in northwest Africa, the Middle East, the Arabian Peninsula, and on Socotra Island in the Indian Ocean. They specialize in burrowing through loose, sandy soil and are roughly triangular in cross-section. Their burrows are the same shape. Short-headed worm lizards do not autotomize

their tails. They use them when they burrow to brace themselves as they thrust the rest of their body forward. There are six species in four genera. *Pachycalamus brevis* is found only on Socotra. The checkered worm lizard, *Trogonophis weigmanni,* occurs in Morocco, Algeria, and Tunisia. It is a live-bearer and gives birth to between two and five live young after a gestation period of about three months. The total weight of the litter often exceeds that of the mother. Not surprisingly, they breed only every two or three years.

Members of the Bipedidae are unique in having a pair of well-developed, powerful front limbs that they use to start digging their burrow and that also help them crawl across the surface. Three species occur in Mexico: one in Baja California and the other two across the water along the Sonoran coast.

Common name Sooty worm lizard
(black-and-white worm lizard)

Scientific name *Amphisbaenia fuliginosa*

Family   Amphisbaenidae

Suborder   Amphisbaenia

Order   Squamata

Size   From 12 in (30 cm) to 18 in (46 cm)

Key features Skull bony, covered with large plates; body
cylindrical with a shallow fold down either
flank and covered with rings of small, square
scales (annuli); tail short with a blunt end;
one of the more distinctively marked worm
lizards with irregular black markings on a
white or pinkish background

Habits   Burrower; rarely seen on the surface

Breeding   Egg layer

Diet   Invertebrates; occasionally small vertebrates

Habitat   Rain forests, forest clearings

Distribution Northern South America from southern
Panama to Peru and Bolivia across to Brazil
and north to Venezuela, Guyana, Surinam,
French Guyana, and the island of Trinidad

Status   Common in suitable habitat

Similar species None; the other large worm lizard in the
region is *Amphisbaenia alba*, which lacks the
black markings; distinguishable from snakes
by the annular arrangement of scales and the
lack of functional eyes

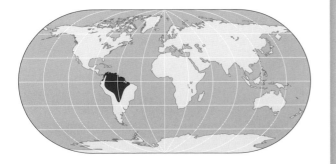

Sooty Worm Lizard

Amphisbaenia fuliginosa

*The sooty worm lizard is one of the most
distinctive amphisbaenians and the one
most likely to be seen in the forests of
northern South America.*

THE SOOTY WORM LIZARD can grow as thick as a
man's thumb, and its powerful jaws can give
quite a bite. It lives in the ground under a layer
of leaf litter and soil, but details of its life are
largely a mystery. Throughout South America it
is perhaps the most common worm lizard (or at
least the one that is seen most commonly).

It lives in all types of habitats except closed-
canopy forests and lowland forests that become
flooded during the rainy season. It turns up
most often on roads that cross grazing pasture,
cultivated fields, and secondary forests (forests
that have sprung up in areas that were formerly
cleared). In Trinidad, where these worm lizards
are also common, they sometimes live in piles
of weathered sawdust in lumber yards. The
sawdust is often infested with grubs of large
wood-boring beetles that find the decaying
wood chips an ideal microhabitat in which to
lay their eggs, and the worm lizards eat the
grubs. More natural habitats include the edges
of forests and forest clearings.

Caterpillar Crawl

It is one of the few species of worm lizard that
is sometimes found on the surface. It moves
across the ground in a caterpillar crawl—lifting
part of its body off the ground slightly and
pulling it forward with the part in front, which
is anchored to the ground. When the moving
part reaches the end of its journey, it is lowered
to the ground and provides leverage to pull the
next section forward. It is not an efficient form
of locomotion—sooty worm lizards make slow
progress compared with, say, heavy-bodied
snakes such as puff adders, *Bitis arietans,* and

others that move in straight lines. Snakes, of course, have a row of wide scales on their underside to help with locomotion.

Sooty worm lizards sometimes turn up in the nests of leaf-cutter ants, *Atta*, which also favor clearings. The maintenance of suitable temperature and humidity levels can be safely left to the insects. The closely related white worm lizard, *Amphisbaenia alba* (whose range overlaps that of the sooty worm lizard, and that also uses leaf-cutter ants' nests as natural incubators), lays clutches of eight to 16 eggs. The smallest sooty worm lizards found so far measured about 4 to 5 inches (10–13 cm) long.

Despite their size, sooty worm lizards eat mostly small prey. The stomachs of museum specimens contain predominantly ants and termites. No doubt they eat them because the insects occur in such large numbers in one place: The effort spent in searching for them is negligible. They are not at all fussy in their diet, however, and earthworms, centipedes, beetles, and insect larvae have also been found in their stomachs. Captives will feed on mealworms, small mice, and even pieces of chopped meat.

They have powerful jaws and sharp teeth. Their only means of defense is to fight off a predator or to intimidate it. To do this, the worm lizard holds its body in a semicircle while raising its tail and head and waving them around. The purpose of this behavior is to fool the predator into attacking the tail instead of the head (as occurs in a number of blunt-tailed, burrowing snakes such as the sand boas, *Eryx*). Because its head and tail are close to each other in this position, the worm lizard may also be able to bite predators that are rash enough to grab its tail.

Common name Iberian worm lizard
(European worm lizard)

Scientific name *Blanus cinereus*

Family   Amphisbaenidae

Suborder   Amphisbaenia

Order   Squamata

Size   12 in (30 cm) maximum but usually
               considerably smaller

Key features Resembles a purple or brown earthworm,
               but on close examination a mouth and
               vestigial eyes can be seen; head is distinct
               from the body, having an obvious fold of skin
               immediately behind it

Habits   Subterranean burrower

Breeding   Egg layer; clutch consists of a single egg

Diet   Ants, grubs, and other small invertebrates

Habitat   Varied (but avoids compacted soils)

Distribution Southern two-thirds of Spain and Portugal

Status   Probably common in suitable habitats

Similar species None in the region; the Anatolian worm
               lizard, *Blanus strauchii*, is found on the islands
               and mainland of the eastern Mediterranean
               and into the Middle East; it lacks the
               prominent fold of skin behind the head

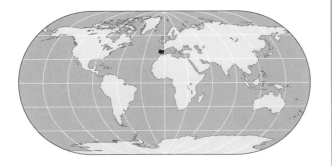

Iberian Worm Lizard

Blanus cinereus

*The Iberian worm lizard is the only worm lizard on the
European mainland. Together with a few close
relatives, it is widely separated from the other
members of its family.*

THE GENUS *BLANUS* contains only three or four
species. Two live along the shores and inland
mountains of North Africa. They are *B. mettetali*
and *B. tingitanus*, although the latter is
pratically indistinguishable from the Iberian
worm lizard. The Anatolian worm lizard,
B. strauchii, lives on a few Greek islands, on
mainland Turkey, in northern Iraq, and in Syria.
Between these populations and the rest of the
African worm lizards is a gap of several
thousand miles; they probably became
separated from the rest of the family when the
continent began to dry out, and the Sahara
Desert formed. The *Blanus* species are thought
to be the most primitive worm lizards, having
only one body ring (annulus) per vertebra,
while the others all have two. They have no
specialized burrowing technique—they just use
their rigid skull to push through loose soil.

Daytime Retreats

Iberian worm lizards do most of their burrowing
in the spring when the ground is moist and
friable (crumbly). By midsummer the soil is dry
and baked and too hard for making tunnels. At
that time of the year they retreat to lower levels
during the day but may come up to the surface
under stones at night, perhaps basking in the
heat that is retained there. They can also be
found under stones early in the morning. If they
are disturbed when they are cold, they remain
rigid and are easily picked up; but when they
have warmed up, they are quick to retreat
down a tunnel. Given the right kind of soil, they
can live in almost any habitat—open pine
forests, fields, roadside embankments, and the

American Cousin

The Florida worm lizard, *Rhineura floridana*, is another species that is widely separated from its nearest relatives. It is sometimes placed in a family of its own, the Rhineuridae, but other herpetologists include it within the Amphisbaenidae. This species, which grows to about 16 inches (41 cm), lives in well-drained, sandy soils in pine and broad-leaf hammocks in north and central Florida. It has no pigment and looks like a thin earthworm. Its mouth is countersunk, its tail is flattened from the top, and it has a patch of slightly rough scales on its upper surface that presumably help it push against the soil when it burrows. Its biology is virtually unknown. It lays one to three eggs in the summer. They hatch in early fall, and the young probably eat termites and other soft-bodied invertebrates. It appears to be the sole survivor of a group of worm lizards that were formerly common and widespread in North America, where a number of fossils of this and similar species have been found.

⊕ *The Florida worm lizard,* Rhineura floridana, *is the sole living member of its family with an extensive fossil record across North America.*

compacted sand between dunes. They occur up to about 6,000 feet (1,828 m).

They are rarely seen on the surface except during heavy rain at night and are most often turned up accidentally during digging or plowing. Mechanized plowing has dramatically reduced numbers of worm lizards living in flat, open habitats. Worm lizards brought to the surface during the day are often seen and eaten by a wide range of predators such as snakes and small birds of prey. Toads probably eat them at night.

They feed on ants, including their larvae and pupae, caterpillars, beetle grubs, and crawling insects, which they locate by the minute sounds they make when they move around. From the numbers of gravid females found at any one time, it seems that they breed only every two or three years. Known clutches consist of a single, elongated egg.

⊖ *The Iberian worm lizard's head is small and triangular. Its tiny eyes lie beneath translucent scales, and a fold of skin separates the head from the body.*

109

Common name Ajolote (mole lizard, Mexican worm lizard)

Scientific name *Bipes biporus*

Family Bipedidae

Suborder Amphisbaenia

Order Squamata

Size From 7 in (18 cm) to 9 in (23 cm)

Key features Resembles a long earthworm with two front legs; legs are situated very far forward just behind the head and are thick and powerful like those of a mole; body has little or no pigment and is pinkish white; the vestigial eyes and the body rings show up well; a shallow groove runs along its flanks

Habits Subterranean, only rarely appearing on the surface

Breeding Egg layer; female lays 1–4 eggs in summer; eggs hatch after about 2 months

Diet Small invertebrates, especially termites and their larvae; also larger animals, such as small lizards

Habitat Dry, sandy plains, often with scattered bushes

Distribution Baja California, Mexico

Status Very common in suitable habitats

Similar species 2 other species of *Bipes* live in mainland Mexico

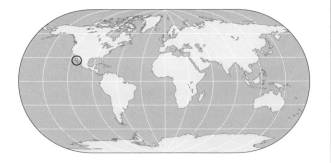

Ajolote

Bipes biporus

The ajolotes of Mexico are unique in being the only worm lizards with legs. They use them for dragging their bodies across the surface and for starting their burrows.

AJOLOTES ARE UNMISTAKABLE in appearance. They resemble an earthworm with two powerful front legs. Each leg ends in a foot that has five long, strong claws, giving the creature the alternative common name of mole lizard.

There are three species in the genus *Bipes*, all with two legs, all in Mexico, and all capable of discarding their tails. Until 1970 there were fewer than 50 specimens of all three species in the world's museums; by the end of a thorough study published in 1982 a total of more than 3,800 had been collected!

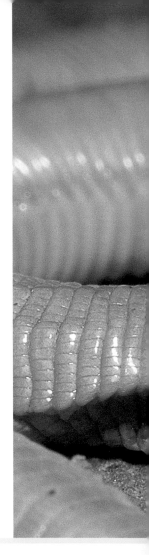

Bipes and the Origins of Baja California

The distribution of the three species of *Bipes* tells us a lot about the geological history of the region in which they live. *Bipes biporus* is found only on the Baja California peninsula. The other two species, *B. canaliculatus* and *B. tridactylus* (with no common names of their own), live along the west coast of mainland Mexico. The ajolotes' distribution patterns, together with geological evidence, help us understand the origins of the peninsula. Originally the southern half of the Baja peninsula was part of the Mexican mainland. Later it broke away from what is now Sonora along a north-south fault line and drifted west and north, taking *Bipes* and other Sonoran species with it (including rosy boas, *Charina trivirgata*, for instance). Eventually it collided with an underwater landmass and lodged as an island off the Mexican coast. Later, volcanic activity in central Baja caused the land to uplift, and the "new" part of Baja California was joined to the "old" northern section. Looking at a map of Mexico, it is easy to see how the southern part of the peninsula would have fitted neatly along the coast near the place where the two mainland *Bipes* species live today.

Monstrous Name

The ajolote gets its name from the same origins as the axolotl (Mexican mole salamander), *Ambystoma mexicanum*. Both are Aztec in origin, and both sound much the same when pronounced in Spanish. The names tend to be interchangeable: The axolotl is sometimes referred to as "ajolote" in literature. Xolotl was the disfigured twin brother of Quetzalcóatl (an Aztec deity), and the word came to mean monster. To people living in Baja California the ajolote is regarded with some degree of fear and superstition.

Snatching Prey

The ajolote is a voracious predator. It ambushes surface-dwelling invertebrates and small vertebrates, dragging them into its tunnels, where it crushes them and tears them apart using its powerful jaws. In warm weather ajolotes are usually found within 2 inches (5 cm) of the surface, ready to break through if they sense prey above. In colder weather they go deeper, up to 8 inches (20 cm), but they remain active throughout the year.

As the human population of Baja California increases, ajolotes are seen more often. They frequently turn up in plant pots, having been accidentally introduced along with a shovelful of soil. They may even emerge in bathrooms as water percolates down into the ground—they have been known to push up the floor tiles from below to reach the surface.

Breeding

Females lay small clutches of eggs in June or July, which hatch about two months later at the beginning of the summer rains. The hatchlings measure about 5 inches (13 cm) in length, but details of their early life and their growth rate are sadly lacking. It seems that females breed only every two years; together with a small clutch size, this indicates that recruitment rates are low and that adult ajolotes probably live for a number of years.

⊕ *Unlike other worm lizards, the ajolote has prominent front legs. Their position well forward on its body, close to its head has given rise to a folk name, lagartija con orejas ("little lizard with ears").*

The collection was achieved by an army of helpers with shovels who dug holes at regular intervals as they walked across the land. Ajolotes and their close relatives were found to be far more numerous than anyone had previously thought.

Bipes biporus from the southern half of Baja California is by far the most common and widespread of the three species. It lives in dry, sandy soil, and its tunnel systems are often centered on the bases of fence posts, where termites are also common.

Glossary

Words in SMALL CAPITALS refer to other entries in the glossary.

Acrodont (teeth) teeth attached to the upper edge of the jaw, as opposed to the inside surface (PLEURODONT) or in sockets (THECODONT)

Adaptation a characteristic shape, behavior, or physiological process that equips an organism (or group of related organisms) for its way of life and habitat

Advanced relatively recently evolved (opposite of "primitive")

Albino an animal that has no color pigment in its body and has red eyes

Amniotic egg an egg with a fluid-filled sac within a membrane that encloses the embryo of reptiles, birds, and mammals. Animals that produce amniotic eggs are known as amniotes

Amplexus the position adopted during mating in most frogs and many salamanders, in which the male clasps the female with one or both pairs of limbs. See AXILLARY AMPLEXUS and INGUINAL AMPLEXUS

Annuli the growth rings often visible on the shell of CHELONIANS

Anterior the front part or head and shoulders of an animal

Aposematic coloration bright coloration serving to warn a potential predator that an animal is distasteful or poisonous

Arboreal living in trees or shrubs

Autotomy self-amputation of part of the body. Some lizards practice CAUDAL autotomy: They discard all or part of their tail

Axillary amplexus mating position in frogs in which the male grasps the female behind her front limbs. See INGUINAL AMPLEXUS

Barbel a small, elongated "feeler," or sensory process, on the head, usually of aquatic animals, e.g., some pipid frogs

Binocular vision the ability to focus both eyes on a single subject. The eyes must point forward (not sideways as in most reptiles and amphibians). Binocular vision enables animals, including humans, to judge distances

Bridges the sides of a turtle's shell, attaching to the CARAPACE above and the PLASTRON below

Brille the transparent covering over the eyes of snakes and some lizards, such as geckos

Bromeliad member of a family of plants restricted to the New World. Many live attached to trees, including "urn plants" in which ARBOREAL frogs sometimes breed

Calcareous containing calcium carbonate

Carapace the upper part of the shell of turtles and tortoises, the other parts being the PLASTRON and the BRIDGES. Also used to describe the hard structure covering part of any animal's body

Caudal relating to the tail, as in subcaudal scales beneath a snake's tail and caudal (tail) fin

Chelonian a member of the ORDER Chelonia, containing all reptiles variously known as terrapins, turtles, and tortoises

Chromatophore a specialized cell containing pigment, usually located in the outer layers of the skin

Chromosome a thread-shaped structure consisting largely of genetic material (DNA), found in the nucleus of cells

Cirrus (pl. cirri) a slender, usually flexible appendage on an animal

CITES an international conservation organization: Convention on International Trade in Endangered Species

Class a TAXONOMIC category ranking below PHYLUM, containing a number of ORDERS

Cloaca the common chamber into which the urinary, digestive, and reproductive systems discharge their contents, and which opens to the exterior; from Latin meaning "sewer" or "drain"

Clutch the eggs laid by a female at one time

Continuous breeder an animal that may breed at any time of year

Convergent evolution the effect of unrelated animals looking like each other because they have adapted to similar conditions in similar ways

Coprophagy the practice of eating excrement

Costal relating to the ribs

Costal grooves grooves or folds along the flanks of caecilians and some salamanders that correspond to the position of the ribs

Crocodilian a member of the order Crocodylia, including alligators, caimans, crocodiles, and gharials

Cryptic having the ability to remain hidden, usually by means of camouflage, e.g., cryptic coloration

Cutaneous respiration breathing that takes place across the skin's surface, especially important in amphibians

Cycloid disklike, resembling a circle

Denticle toothlike scale

Dermis layer of skin immediately below the EPIDERMIS

Dewlap flap or fold of skin under an animal's throat. Sometimes used in displays, e.g., in anole lizards

Dimorphism the existence of two distinct forms within a SPECIES, which is then said to be dimorphic. In species in which there are more than two forms, they are polymorphic. See SEXUAL DIMORPHISM

Direct development transition from egg to the adult form in amphibians without passing through a free-living LARVAL stage

Dorsal relating to the back or upper surface of the body or one of its parts

Ectotherm (adj. ectothermic) an animal that relies on external heat sources, such as the sun, to raise its body temperature. Reptiles and amphibians are ectotherms. See ENDOTHERM

Eft juvenile, TERRESTRIAL phase in the life cycle of a newt. The red eft is the terrestrial juvenile form of the eastern newt, *Notophthalmus viridescens*

Egg tooth small toothlike scale that some amphibians and reptiles have on the tip of the snout to assist in breaking through their eggshell

Endemic SPECIES, GENERA, or FAMILIES that are restricted to a particular geographical region

Endotherm (adj. endothermic) an animal that can sustain a high body temperature by means of heat generated within the body by the metabolism. See ECTOTHERM

Epidermis surface layer of the skin of a vertebrate

Epiphyte plant growing on another plant but not a parasite. Includes many orchids and BROMELIADS and some mosses and ferns

Estivation a state of inactivity during prolonged periods of drought or high temperature. During estivation the animal often buries itself in soil or mud. See HIBERNATION

Estuarine living in the lower part of a river (estuary) where fresh water meets and mixes with seawater

Explosive breeder a SPECIES in which the breeding season is very short, resulting in large numbers of animals mating at the same time

External fertilization fusing of eggs and sperm outside the female's body, as in nearly all frogs and toads. See INTERNAL FERTILIZATION

Family TAXONOMIC category ranking below ORDER, containing GENERA that are more closely related to one another than any other grouping of genera

Farming hatching and rearing of young CHELONIANS and CROCODILIANS from a captive-breeding population. See RANCHING

Fauna the animal life of a locality or region

Femoral gland gland situated on an animal's thigh

Femoral pores row of pores along an animal's thighs. Most obvious in many lizards

Fertilization union of an egg and a sperm

Gamete OVUM or sperm

Genus (pl. genera) taxonomic category ranking below FAMILY; a group of SPECIES all more closely related to one another than to any other group of species

Gestation carrying the developing young within the body. Gestation period is the length of time that this occurs

Gill respiratory structure in aquatic animals through which gas exchange takes place

Gill slits slits in which GILLS are situated and present in some amphibians and their LARVAE

Granular (scale) small grainlike scales covering the body, as in some geckos and in the file snakes, *Acrochordus*

Gravid carrying eggs or young

Gular pouch area of expandable skin in the throat region

Hedonic glands glands in a male salamander that stimulate a female when they are rubbed against her body

Heliotherm an animal that basks to regulate body temperature

Hemipenis (pl. hemipenes) one of two grooved copulatory structures present in the males of some reptiles

Herbivore animal that eats plants

Heterogeneous (scales) scales that differ in shape or size. See HOMOGENEOUS (SCALES)

Hibernation a period of inactivity, often spent underground, to avoid extremes of cold. See ESTIVATION

Hinge a means by which the PLASTRON of some CHELONIANS can be pulled up, giving the reptile more protection against a would-be predator

Home range an area in which an animal lives except for MIGRATIONS or rare excursions

Homogeneous (scales) scales that are all the same shape and size. See HETEROGENEOUS (SCALES)

Hyoid "u"-shaped bone at the base of the tongue to which the larynx is attached

Inguinal pertaining to the groin

Inguinal amplexus a mating position in which a male frog or salamander clasps a female around the lower abdomen. See AXILLARY AMPLEXUS

Intergular scute a single plate, or SCUTE, lying between the paired gular scutes on the PLASTRON of side-necked turtles

Internal fertilization fusing of eggs and sperm inside the female's body, as in reptiles and most salamanders. See EXTERNAL FERTILIZATION

Interstitial the thin skin between the scales of reptiles. Sometimes called "interscalar" skin

Introduced species brought from lands where it occurs naturally to lands where it has not previously occurred

IUCN International Union for the Conservation of Nature, responsible for assigning animals and plants to internationally agreed categories of rarity. See table below

Jacobson's organ (or vomeronasal organ) one of a pair of grooves extending from the nasal cavity and opening into the mouth cavity in some mammals and reptiles. Molecules collected on the tongue are sampled by this organ, which supplements the sense of smell

Juvenile young animal, not sexually mature

Karst a porous form of limestone

Keeled scales a ridge on the DORSAL scales of some snakes

Keratophagy the practice of eating molted skin

Lamella (pl. lamellae) thin transverse plates across the undersides of the toes of some lizards, especially geckos

Larva (pl. larvae) early stage in the development of an animal (including amphibians) after hatching from the egg

Lateral line organ sense organ embedded in the skin of some aquatic animals, including LARVAL salamanders and some frogs, which responds to waterborne vibrations. Usually arranged in a row along the animal's side

Leucistic an animal that lacks all pigment except that in its eyes. Partially leucistic animals have patches of white over an otherwise normally pigmented skin. See ALBINO

Life cycle complete life history of an organism from one stage to the recurrence of that stage, e.g., egg to egg

Life history history of a single individual organism from the fertilization of the egg until its death

Lifestyle general mode of life of an animal, e.g., NOCTURNAL predator, aquatic HERBIVORE, parasite

Live-bearing giving birth to young that have developed beyond the egg stage. Live-bearers may be VIVIPAROUS or OVOVIVIPAROUS

Lure (noun) part of the body, such as the tail, that is used to entice prey closer

Mental gland gland on the chin of some newts and salamanders that appears to stimulate the female during courtship; one of the HEDONIC GLANDS

Metabolism chemical or energy changes occurring within a living organism that are involved in various life activities

Metamorphosis transformation of an animal from one stage of its life history to another, e.g., from LARVA to adult

Microenvironment local conditions that immediately surround an organism

Migration movement of animals from one place to another, often in large numbers and often for breeding purposes

Mimic an animal that resembles an animal belonging to another SPECIES, usually a distasteful or venomous one, or some inedible object

Milt sperm-containing fluid produced by a male frog during egg laying to fertilize the eggs

Montane pertaining to mountains or SPECIES that live in mountains

Morph form or phase of an animal

Morphological relating to the form and structure of an organism

Nasolabial groove a groove running from the nostril to the upper lip in male plethodontid salamanders

Neonate the newborn young of a live-bearer

Neoteny condition in which a LARVA fails to METAMORPHOSE and retains its larval features as an adult. Species with this condition are said to be neotenic. The axolotl is the best-known example. See PEDOMORPHOSIS

Neotropics the tropical part of the New World, including northern South America, Central America, part of Mexico, and the West Indies

Newt amphibious salamanders of the genera *Triturus, Taricha,* and *Notophthalmus*

Niche the role played by a SPECIES in its particular community. It is determined by its food and temperature preferences; each species' niche within a community is unique

Nocturnal active at night

Nuptial pad an area of dark, rough skin that develops in male amphibians on the hands, arms, or chest of some SPECIES prior to the breeding season. Its purpose is to allow the male to grip the female in AMPLEXUS

Occipital lobe the pyramid-shaped area at the back of the brain that helps an animal interpret vision

Ocular of the eye

Olfactory relating to the sense of smell

Omnivore an animal that eats both animal and plant material

Order taxonomic category ranking below CLASS and above FAMILY

Osteoderm small bone in the skin of some reptiles; lies under the scales

Ovary female gonad or reproductive organ that produces the OVUM

Overwinter survive the winter

Oviduct the duct in females that carries the OVUM from the ovary to the CLOACA

Oviparous reproducing by eggs that hatch outside the female's body

IUCN CATEGORIES

EX Extinct, when there is no reasonable doubt that the last individual of the species has died.

EW Extinct in the Wild, when a species is known only to survive in captivity or as a naturalized population well outside the past range.

CR Critically Endangered, when a species is facing an extremely high risk of extinction in the wild in the immediate future.

EN Endangered, when a species is facing a very high risk of extinction in the wild in the near future.

VU Vulnerable, when a species is facing a high risk of extinction in the wild in the medium-term future.

LR Lower Risk, when a species has been evaluated and does not satisfy the criteria for CR, EN, or VU.

DD Data Deficient, when there is not enough information about a species to assess the risk of extinction.

NE Not Evaluated, species that have not been assessed by the IUCN criteria.

Picture Credits

Abbreviations

A Ardea, London; BCL Bruce Coleman Limited; CM Chris Mattison; FLPA Frank Lane Picture Agency; NHPA Natural History Photographic Agency; NPL Naturepl.com; PW Premaphotos Wildlife; P.com/OSF Photolibrary.com/Oxford Scientific Films; SPL Science Photo Library

t = top; **b** = bottom; **c** = center; **l** = left; **r** = right

Jacket: tl Geoff Trinder/A; **tr** Martin Harvey/NHPA; **bl** John Cancalosi/A; **br** Marty Cordano/P.com/OSF

8-9 James Carmichael jr./NHPA; **10** Ken Griffiths/NHPA; **11** Bruce Davidson/NPL; **12, 12–13** CM; **13** Waina Cheng/P.com/OSF; **14–15** Barry Mansell/NPL; **17** Daniel Heuclin/NHPA; **18** Marian Bacon, A/P.com/OSF; **18–19** Michael Dick, AA/P.com/OSF; **20–21**CM; **21t** Daniel Heuclin/NHPA; **22–23** Nick Upton/NPL; **25** Kathie Atkinson/P.com/OSF; **27** CM; **29** P.com/OSF; **31, 32–33** Anthony Bannister/NHPA; **35, 37** CM; **38–39** Richard Kirby/P.com/OSF; **41** Michael Fogden/P.com/OSF; **42–43** Steven D.Miller/NPL; **43** Otto Rogge, A.N.T. Photo Library/NHPA; **45** John Cancalosi/NPL; **46** Bert & Babs Wells/P.com/OSF; **46–47** Katie Atkinson/P.com/OSF; **49** Eric Lindgren/A; **51** AA/P.com/OSF; **53** P.com/OSF; **54–55** Haroldo Palo jr./NHPA; **57** Mark Bowler/NHPA; **58–59** Laurie Campbell/NHPA; **59** Tony Phelps/NPL; **61** Brian Kenney/P.com/OSF; **63** Daniel Heuclin/NHPA; **65** P.com/OSF; **67** Michael Fogden/P.com/OSF; **69** P.com/OSF; **71** Brian Kenney/P.com/OSF; **73** Kennith W. Fink/A; **75** Joe McDonald, AA/P.com/OSF; **77** Daniel Heuclin/NHPA; **78–79, 81** Daniel Heuclin/NHPA; **83** Alan Root, SAL/P.com/OSF; **84–85** Stan Osolinski/P.com/OSF; **85** Tony Heald/NPL; **87** Brian Kenney/P.com/OSF; **88–89** Bernard Castelein/NPL; **89** CM; **90–91** D.Zingel Eichhorn/FLPA; **93** ANT Photo Library/NHPA; **95** Adrian Warren/A; **96** Michael Pitts/NPL; **97** Jurgen Freund/NPL; **99** Mark Deeble & Victoria Stone/P.com/OSF; **101** Alain Compost; **103** Anthony Bannister/NHPA; **104–105** CM; **105** Jany Sauvanet/NHPA; **107** CM; **108–109** Jorge Sierra/P.com/OSF; **109** David M. Dennis/P.com/OSF; **111** CM